JOURNAL FOR THE STUDY OF THE OLD TESTAMENT
SUPPLEMENT SERIES

61

Editors
David J A Clines
Philip R Davies

JSOT Press
Sheffield

From CHAOS to RESTORATION

An Integrative Reading of Isaiah 24–27

Dan G. Johnson

Journal for the Study of the Old Testament
Supplement Series 61

Published by JSOT Press
JSOT Press is an imprint of
Sheffield Academic Press Ltd
The University of Sheffield
343 Fulwood Road
Sheffield S10 3BP
England

Typeset by Sheffield Academic Press
and
printed in Great Britain
by Billing & Sons Ltd
Worcester

British Library Cataloguing in Publication Data

Johnson, Dan G.
From chaos to restoration.
1. Bible. O.T. Isaiah XXIV - XXVII. Critical studies
I. Title II. Series
224'.106

ISBN 1-85075-112-9
ISBN 1-85075-061-0 Pbk

CONTENTS

PREFACE

I wish to acknowledge my gratitude to several friends and teachers who have encouraged and guided me through this study of Isaiah 24–27. Dr Bernhard W. Anderson first introduced me to these obscure chapters in a seminar entitled 'From Prophecy to Apocalyptic'. His support and wise counsel saw me through the early stages of research. I owe much to Dr Ben Ollenburger, who, through his expertise in the study of early apocalyptic literature, was able to provide numerous suggestions, particularly with regard to bibliographical data. For extensive emotional support and exemplary scholarship throughout my program I am grateful to Dr Katherine Sakenfeld. My chief debt of gratitude is to Dr J.J.M. Roberts, my adviser. His probing questions, insightful criticisms, and patient manner have contributed greatly to this study. Finally, to those friends, both known and unknown, who provided financial support during these four years of study, I express deep appreciation.

ABBREVIATIONS

AARSR	American Academy of Religion, Studies in Religion
AB	The Anchor Bible
ALBO	Analecta lovaniensia biblica et orientalia
AThANT	Abhandlungen zur Theologie des Alten und Neuen Testaments
BAT	Die Botschaft des Alten Testaments
BDB	Brown, Driver, Briggs, A Hebrew and English Lexicon of the Old Testament
BHS	Biblica Hebraica, Stuttgartensia
BHT	Beiträge zur historischen Theologie
BKAT	Biblischer Kommentar: Altes Testament
BO	Biblia et Orientalia
BWANT	Beiträge zur Wissenschaft vom Alten und Neuen Testament
BZAT	Beiträge zur alttestamentliche Theologie
BZAW	Beihefte zur Zeitschrift für die alttestamentliche Wissenschaft
CBQ	*Catholic Biblical Quarterly*
CRB	Cahiers de la revue biblique
CTA	Corpus des tablettes en cunéiformes alphabétiques
ET	*The Expository Times*
ETR	Etudes théologiques et religieuses
FRLANT	Forschungen zur Religion und Literatur des Alten und Neuen Testaments
G-K	Gesenius-Kautzsch, Hebrew Grammar
HKAT	Handkommentar zum Alten Testament
HSM	Harvard Semitic Monographs
ICC	The International Critical Commentary on the Holy Scriptures of the Old and New Testaments
IDB	*The Interpreter's Dictionary of the Bible*
IDBS	*The Interpreter's Dictionary of the Bible, Supplement*
JAAR	*Journal of the American Academy of Religion*
JAOS	*Journal of the American Oriental Society*
JB	The Jerusalem Bible

JBL	*Journal of Biblical Literature*
JPS	Jewish Publication Society
JThS	*Journal of Theological Studies*
KAT	Kommentar zum Alten Testament
KBL	*Koehler–Baumgartner, Lexikon zum Alten Testament*
LXX	Septuagint
NEB	The New English Bible
NIC	New International Commentary
NIV	The New International Version
OJRS	*Ohio Journal of Religious Studies*
OTL	Old Testament Library
PSB	*Princeton Seminary Bulletin*
RQ	*Restoration Quarterly*
SBT	Studies in Biblical Theology
SEÅ	*Svensk exegetisk årsbok*
SJT	*Scottish Journal of Theology*
ST	*Studia Theologica*
Symm	Symmachus
TBC	Torch Bible Commentaries
Theod	Theodotian
ThZ	*Theologische Zeitschrift*
UT	Ugaritic Textbook
Vg	Vulgate
VT	*Vetus Testamentum*
VTS	Vetus Testamentum Supplement
ZAW	*Zeitschrift für die alttestamentliche Wissenschaft*
ZThK	*Zeitschrift für Theologie und Kirche*
ZWTh	*Zeitschrift für wissenschaftliche Theologie*

Chapter 1

INTRODUCTION

It is no secret that in recent years biblical scholars have reinstated apocalyptic as a major force in the development of Biblical Theology.[1] Concomitant with this renaissance of interest in all things apocalyptic has been the assertion that the origin of apocalyptic is not to be found in extra-biblical realms, but rather in the Old Testament itself, and particularly in the area of prophetic eschatology.[2] To be more precise, it has become the *communis opinio* that the initial transformation of prophetic eschatology into what would eventually become full-blown apocalyptic is to be found in Isaiah 24–27, the so-called Isaianic apocalypse, and a few other passages.[3]

While such recent developments are to be welcomed as providing significant contributions to the area of biblical studies, it is nevertheless ironic that Isa. 24–27 should be given such a seminal role in the development of apocalyptic, since there is, as yet, no clear consensus regarding the basic meaning of this pivotal portion of the Old Testament. There continues to be widespread disagreement of such basic matters as (A) the date of the composition and the identity of the city (or cities),[4] (B) the structure of these four chapters, and (C) the perspective of Isa. 24–27. Until these and other issues are resolved, not only will the alleged association between Isa. 24–27 and the origin of apocalyptic continue to be purely speculative, but also a significant portion of scripture will remain lost to the church and synagogue.

A. *Date and Identification of the City (or Cities)*

With the arrival of the critical era came also the abandonment of an eighth-century, Isaianic authorship for Isa. 24–27.[5] Similarly, at the other end of the continuum, the discovery of the Dead Sea Scrolls, including a complete Isaiah scroll dating from approximately 150 BCE,[6] rendered impossible the second-century dates proposed by Duhm and Procksch.[7] It is a testimony to the obscurity of Isa. 24–27 that most of the intervening centuries have found one or more adherents.

E.S. Mulder and O. Eissfeldt were drawn to the reference to Moab in 25.10b, and suggested the destruction of a Moabite city in the third century as the occasion for this composition.[8] But most scholars have recognized the Moab pericope (25.10b-12) as a polemical intrusion into the text which has nothing to do with its context and is uncharacteristic of the rest of the composition; it is to be excised. W. Kessler regards the city of 25.2 and 26.5, 6 as destroyed by Demetrius Poliorketes in 296, he assigns a third-century date to 25.2 and 26.5, 6 as well.[9]

Finally, O. Plöger is another interpreter who places Isa. 24–27 in the third century. In arriving at this conclusion, Plöger, unlike most other scholars, has not depended on the identification of the city. He regards the reference to the city in 24.10 as a reference to 'city life . . . in general';[10] 25.2 and 26.5, 6 belong to two independent songs which have no bearing on the interpretation of the composition;[11] similarly the mention of a city in 27.10 belongs to a section which is much older than the rest of the 'Apocalypse' and was only added at a later date.[12] In my judgment, Plöger has argued for a third-century date largely because he viewed Isa. 24–27 through the lens of the book of Daniel. Consequently, he imagined links between the two documents which bolstered the thesis of his book, *Theocracy and Eschatology*. But such links are simply not there.[13]

W. Rudolph correctly determined that since the destruction of the hostile city would have worldwide implications (25.3-10a), there could be only one city intended: Babylon. But because, in his view, the composition celebrated an actual destruction which had already taken place, he ruled out the peaceful overthrow of Babylon by Cyrus in 538, and decided in favor of the devastation of Babylon in 331 by Alexander.[14]

O. Kaiser thinks that all attempts at identifying the city of Isa. 24–27 are misguided since the composition is thoroughly eschatological in nature, looking solely to the 'coming world-wide catastrophe and its effects', with no interest in any particular, historical city.[15] While Kaiser has made a major contribution to the study of Isa. 24–27 by demonstrating that the references to the city are 'pure prophecy',[16] rather than allusions to a past event, I see no reason why the author could not have envisioned the imminent destruction of a particular city. Certainly the author's near obsession with the city throughout the composition would indicate that he has in mind a city that he considers especially evil. On the basis of considerations other than the identity of the city, Kaiser concludes that the composition developed over a period of time between the fourth and second centuries.[17]

Certainly the most thorough work on the identity of the city has been that of J. Lindblom, who maintained that the city was Babylon, and that the composition was written to celebrate the recent destruction of the accursed city at the hands of Zerzes in 485.[18] While his defense of the identity of the city is, for the most part, convincing, he can only defend the date by denying the futuristic thrust of the songs about the city. From the perspective of the composition, the destruction of the city was only prophesied, not described.

H. Wildberger, like Kaiser before him, plays down the significance of any particular city, in light of the eschatological thrust of the composition, seeing the city as a 'Symbol der grossen Gegenmacht Jahwes'.[19] He dates Isa. 24–27 somewhat earlier than Kaiser: between 500 and 400.[20]

Recently, several scholars have argued for a sixth-century provenance. W.E. March, primarily on the basis of his study of the language, located the composition in the period of the exile.[21] He determined that the city in 24.10 was Jerusalem,[22] and that 25.2 and 26.5, 6 did not refer to any particular city, but rather to Yahweh's enemies in general.[23] He excluded 27.2-13 from the composition.[24]

Other support for a sixth-century date has arisen independently of a consideration of the identity of the city. F.M. Cross and two of his students, on the basis of prosodic analysis, have assigned Isa. 24–27 to a period nearly contemporaneous with the exilic document, Second Isaiah.[25] Both P. Hanson and W.R. Millar suggest that the destroyed city is Jerusalem, but they fail to justify this on the basis of a consistent exegesis of the pericopae in which the city is mentioned.[26] Further, though they do not state explicitly that Jerusalem is the referent throughout the composition, they certainly imply it. But in my view, it is highly doubtful that any Jewish writer would rejoice over the destruction of Jerusalem as portrayed in 25.1-5 and 26.5, 6. This is especially true of sixth-century Israel. Even during the highly divisive period when the second temple was destroyed in 70 CE, a period in which one might expect a vitriolic response by the disenfranchised, there is no rejoicing at the destruction.[27]

It is obvious from this brief survey that the trend in recent years has been to place the date of Isa. 24–27 much earlier than the previous generations of scholars had done, to the period of the sixth to the fifth centuries,[28] though within this 200 year span there is still no consensus. With regard to the identity of the city, the lack of agreement is as pervasive as ever.

B. *The Structure of Isaiah 24–27*

Since Duhm's groundbreaking analysis it has become commonplace to divide the composition into two parts: (1) eschatological prophecies or apocalypses and (2) songs about the destruction of a particular city.[29] While Duhm believed this division was evidence against the unity of the composition, other scholars sensed that these chapters were more than a haphazard collection of unrelated parts. G. Hylmö maintained that the pattern of alternation between prophecy and song suggests that chs. 25–26 form a prophetic liturgy.[30] J. Lindblom was greatly influenced by Hylmö's proposal, though he ultimately rejected the appellation, 'prophetic liturgy'. He reasoned (correctly) that (1) the entirety of chs. 24–27 showed signs of integrity, and that it was inappropriate to isolate only chs. 25–26; (2) even chs. 25–26 do not accord with a strict definition of liturgy.[31] Lindblom chose instead to designate Isa. 24–27 a 'Cantata', which was to be sung antiphonally by the Jewish community in celebration of the destruction of the enemy city.[32] G. Fohrer and W. March have each proposed a modification of this basic pattern, returning, however, to Hylmö's designation of 'liturgy'.[33]

In my view, the works of all four interpreters are procrustean efforts which require either the lopping off of those portions of the composition that do not fit the pattern, or a strained and impossible interpretation of certain pericopae in order to make them accord with the pattern. For example, since 24.21-23; 27.1; and 26.15-19 do not conform to the pattern, Lindblom relegates them to 'secondary additions'. Similarly he designates 24.7-16a and 27.2-11 as 'songs of thanksgiving', though the lament-like language in these pericopae renders such a view impossible.[34]

Kaiser and Wildberger have in large measure escaped the tyranny of the prophecy/song schema by recognizing that Isa. 24–27, in its present form, gives evidence of an ordered composition.[35] However, they posit an extended prehistory, or to use Wildberger's term, a *Wachstumsprozess* behind the present text.[36] Wildberger suggests that the first level of the composition consisted of 24.1-6, 14-20; 26.7-21. Later, at three separate times vv. 7-9, 10-12, 13 were added to 24.1-6. To this 'Grundschicht' were added the eschatological passages (24.21-23; 25.6-8, 9-10a) and later the songs about the destruction of the city (25.1-5; 26.1-6). Finally, the various eschatological fragments which make up ch. 27 were added (27.1, 2-5, 6-11, 12, 13).[37]

In my view there are two points which raise serious questions about the whole notion of a *Wachstumsprozess*. (1) Among the various scholars who subscribe to it, there is no agreement as to (a) the isolation of the units, (b) the order in which the units were added, or (c) the motivation behind a particular addition.[38] The subjectivity involved is extreme. (2) I find it difficult to imagine that the choppy and irregular growth process which Wildberger and others allege these chapters underwent could have resulted in such a well-ordered composition. While it may be appropriate to speak of a 'growth process' in relation to such works as First Isaiah and parts of Jeremiah that consist of isolated oracles, and that do not remotely resemble an ordered composition, such is not the case with the unified work which comprises Isa. 24–27.[39]

Once again, this survey has revealed that there is only limited agreement as to the structure of Isa. 24–27. Nevertheless, there has been significant advance since the analysis of Duhm which denied any unity to the composition. And regardless of how one views the prehistory of these chapters, one may with some confidence speak of the compositional unity of Isa. 24–27 in its present form.

C. *The Perspective of the Composition*

A second ramification of Duhm's analysis which separated the songs from their eschatological context was the widespread assumption that the songs referred to a *past* rather than a future event. Even Lindblom, who maintained the basic unity of the composition, thought the songs referred to the recent destruction of the hostile city. But we note that in order for him to hold this view it was necessary to excise the futuristic formulae in 26.1 and 27.2, and to regard as a secondary addition the eschatological passage, 24.21-23, which introduces the song in 25.1-5.[40]

Rudolph was one of the first critical scholars to maintain that the songs, as well as the eschatological oracles, were predictive, referring to a future event.[41] More recently, Plöger, Kaiser, and Wildberger have maintained that Isa. 24–27 is an eschatological document which anticipates the imminent epiphany of Yahweh. Plöger, perhaps as a concession to the influence of Duhm, excluded the songs, which he believed referred to past events; they are later additions which are to be interpreted independently of the rest of the composition.[42] Kaiser and Wildberger agree that in the final form of the text, the songs do not refer to any particular, historical event in the future but symbolize rather the ungodly powers which Yahweh will soon destroy.[43]

The emerging consensus regarding the perspective of Isa. 24–27 is that it is futuristic. However, there is disagreement as to whether the author's purview leaves the realm of history altogether, as Kaiser and Wildberger allege, or whether he anticipates the imminent destruction of a specific city which will introduce the new, eschatological age.

D. *A New Proposal*

After nearly a century of intense critical study of Isa. 24–27, the number of ambiguities and uncertainties regarding these chapters continues to be legion. Yet there appears to be a convergence of viewpoints in several crucial areas: (1) There is general agreement that chs. 24–27 are to be dated early rather than late, closer to the time of the exile than to the book of Daniel. This earlier dating should allow the composition to be interpreted on its own merit, rather than through the lens of the book of Daniel as earlier interpreters were prone to do. (2) There is an emerging consensus that Isa. 24–27 is an ordered composition. (3) There is a growing recognition that the perspective of the composition is futuristic. The referent for the songs lies in the future.[44]

In my judgment, these significant advances have set the stage for a fresh interpretation of Isa. 24–27. I will argue that the composition is comprised of three major parts. Section A (24.1-20), which employs the language of lament, was written on the eve of the destruction of Jerusalem in 587. Because this devastating blow and the ensuing exile were seen as the return to chaos, the poet limned his prediction in the cosmic language of the chaos myth. Section B (24.21–27.1) is an announcement of the imminent victory of Yahweh. It was added later, during the exile when the prophet looked to the future destruction of the city of oppression: Babylon (25.2; 26.5, 6). This mighty (historical) act of Yahweh would mean the national resurrection of Israel and the inauguration of the eschatological age. In section C (27.2-13), the prophet brings the notion of the triumph of Yahweh to its logical conclusion with the theme of the reunification of Israel. Like Jeremiah and Ezekiel, this exilic prophet believed that the reign of Yahweh would reach its consummation only with the restoration of the nation.[45]

Chapter 2

THE RETURN TO CHAOS (ISAIAH 24.1-20)

A. *The Judgment of Yahweh (24.1-13)*

1. *The Determination of the Unit*

There is general agreement that in its present form the first unit terminates with v. 13.[1] This conclusion is supported by the summarizing tone of v. 13 and the sudden shift from the plaintive phrasing in vv. 4-13 to the hymnic expressions of joy in vv. 14-16a.

W.E. March takes exception to this view arguing that the unit extends through v. 15 for the following reasons: (1) IsaQ[a] has a definite break after v. 15.[2] (2) He suggests that, 'The last line of 15 is obviously climactic in tone and provides a proper note on which to conclude a unit'.[3] (3) He considers the *Gattung* to be a lament, and this requires a response of praise by the people, which is expressed in vv. 14, 15.[4]

But there are serious problems with this view: (1) There may be numerous causes of a break in a manuscript. The text at v. 15 shows serious corruption,[5] so the break may be simply the reult of a scribal error. More importantly, from a text-critical point of view, none of the other versions reflects this break after v. 15. That the more decisive break is after v. 13 rather than after v. 15 is supported by W.R. Millar, who notes, 'The lifting up of the voice (*yś'w qwlm*) to shout is a common device familiar from Ugaritic sources to indicate a break or shift in the poem'.[6] (2) I am not convinced that v. 15 is as 'obviously climactic' as is, for example, v. 16a. (3) March is correct in noting the lament-like tone of vv. 4-12, but he has done an injustice to the individual creativity of the author by rigidly imposing on this material the *Gattung* of lament in its strictest form. Rather, the material gives evidence that the author has adapted various forms to suit his particular purposes. (4) Finally, March's explanation of the relationship between vv. 14-15 and the preceding material is hardly satisfactory and only confirms our suspicion of the forced imposition of a *Gattung*: 'The rejoicing . . . reflects the people's belief that, since they had properly made lamentation over their fallen city, God was then committed to come to their aid, to respond favourably as was customary in the communal lamentation ritual'.[7]

2. *The Delimitation of Pericopae with the Unit*

Any discussion of the various pericopae within this unit must be prefaced with the understanding that in the present form of the text, the smaller units have been juxtaposed, modified, and, indeed, transformed to form an integrated composition.[8] The opening unit (vv. 1-13) begins with an announcement of impending judgment (vv. 1-3); this is followed by a description of the devastation of the earth (vv. 4-6) and a particular city (vv. 7-12); and v. 13 concludes the section with a return to the future orientation with which it began. As we shall demonstrate more fully below, the prophet's juxtaposition of the announcement of judgment and the description of the results of that judgment was intentional. Further, though we will recognize a break between vv. 6 and 7, we will also note that the author has intentionally adapted the two separate units in order to mark a progression of focus from the general (the earth) to the particular (the city).

The first pericope finds its terminus with the quotation formula in v. 3b, *ky yhwh dbr 't hdbr hzh*, which in turn follows the *inclusio* formed between *hbwq tbwq*, v. 3, and *bwqq*, v. 1. This view is supported by the change of verb tense in v. 4 from the imperfect to the perfect. Despite these points, several scholars extend the first pericope through v. 6 Lindblom argues for the extension on the basis of consistency of meter throughout the six verses.[9] But the stylistic features which we have mentioned must be given the greater weight.

Wildberger has suggested that the phrase, *ky yhwh dbr 't hdbr hzh* introduces the following word in vv. 4ff.[10] He recognizes that the phrase, *ky yhwh dbr . . .*, stands at the *end* of a section in 22.25 and 25.8, but notes that it initiates a word in 1.2 and Jer. 13.15 (though, in my judgment, the latter reference is questionable).

While his view is certainly possible, and has the advantage of providing a 'word from Yahweh',[11] there are three points which argue against Wildberger's position: (1) Because the author employs the phrase to *conclude* the section, 25.6-8, and because its occurrence here is parallel, we must assume that he understood it as a concluding formula in v. 3 as well. (2) Verses 4ff. seem to be more of a descriptive rather than a prophetic nature. (3) The appeal to Isa. 1.2 has little bearing on this pericope, because the phrase in Isa. 1.2 is followed by a direct address by Yahweh in the first person. There is nothing similar to that in 24.4.

The end of the second pericope is v. 6, as indicated by the following points: (1) The repetition of *ʿl-kn* forms a 'double conclusion'.[12] (2) The focus of these verses is on the earth, while vv. 7ff. center on the city. (3) The phrase, *wnšʾr ʾnwš mzʿr*, is summarizing in tone.

The third pericope focuses on the city beginning with v. 7[13] and concluding with v. 12. While we make a distinction between the two pericopae (vv. 4-6 and 7-12), we recognize that they share a similar tone and vocabulary. Indeed, the fact that v. 7 picks up the terms found in v. 4 suggests that the author has formed the two units into one. The change of tense from the perfect back to the imperfect in v. 13 marks the end of this unit at v. 12.[14]

Verse 13 returns to the futuristic perspective of the opening verses. It would appear that the prophetic predictions of judgment in v. 13 and vv. 1-3a are intended by the author to frame or bracket the intervening description of devastation (vv. 4-12).

3. *The Designation of Gattungen*

It is generally agreed that the first pericope (vv. 1-3) is an announcement of judgment.[15] Even those interpreters who extend it through v. 6 recognize it as such.[16]

With regard to vv. 4-6, there are several differing viewpoints. P.L. Redditt maintains that the form is a 'Threat with Motivation'.[17] But there seems to be little emphasis on motivation. Similarly, Rudolph, Lindblom and Wildberger, as we have seen, have failed to note the shift from the imperfect to the perfect tense, which was surely intentional on the part of the author. Consequently their designation of *Gattung* does not reflect this difference.[18]

In my view, the reference to a breach of covenant, which is connected in a causal relationship (*ʿl-kn*) to the curse which follows, strongly suggests that the author has adapted a covenant law-suit motif. To be sure, not all of the elements of a covenant law-suit are present, for example, the appeal to a third party such as one finds in Isa. 1.2,[19] but the two primary features are present: violation of covenant responsibility and the resultant curse.

The significant study by D.R. Hillers, *Treaty Curses and the Old Testament Prophets*, concludes with a quotation of Isa. 24.5-6.[20] Of the many treaty-curses which he lists, three are of special significance for our study: (1) the removal of joyful sounds—vv. 8, 9, 11;[21] (2) famine—*passim*;[22] (3) lack of men—v. 6.[23] Quite clearly our passage shares the common ancient near eastern view that a broken covenant results in specific curses.

This has brought us to a consideration of vv. 7-12, which, as I have noted, in their present form create a continuous whole with vv. 4-6. P. Lohmann[24] held that vv. 7-12 were a 'profane victory song, a mocking song (Spottlied)'. He suggested that there is no note of lament, but rather, 'ein spöttischer Unterton klingt durch den ganzen Sang'.[25]

J. Lindblom modified Lohmann's proposal slightly because, as he said, a victory song 'doch von den Siegern gesungen werden müsste. Hier sind die Singenden bloss Zuschauer bei der Katastrophe, nicht selbst Teilnähmer'.[26] He designated the form as a 'Klagelied',[27] but insisted that the lament over the fate of a foreign city, when placed in the mouth of rejoicing Jews (vv. 14-16a), becomes a mocking song.[28]

But we must reject both Lohmann's and Lindblom's views for the following three reasons:

(1) Even a cursory comparison of 24.7ff. with the mocking song of Isaiah 47 makes it obvious that 24.7ff. does not qualify as a mocking song. The tone of derision and ridicule that pervades ch. 47 is completely absent from 24.7-12.[29]

(2) The vocabulary suggests that the lament is genuine. For *'bl* and *'mll* note the following texts: Isa. 3.16; 33.9; Jer. 4.28; 12.4, 11; 14.2; 23.10; Hos. 4.3; 10.5; Amos 1.2; 8.8; Lam. 1.4; 2.8; 3.15. All of these references lament a situation of destruction in the land of Israel/Judah, and they are strikingly similar in tone and mood to the references in Isaiah 24. The verb *'nḥ* (v. 7) appears twelve times in the OT. Except for the general reference in Prov. 29.2, this term is always employed in a genuinely lamentable situation (and always with reference to the people of God—a point to be built upon later): Exod. 2.3; Joel 1.18; Ezek. 21.11 (21.6, Eng.); Lam. 1.4, 8, 11, 21. The word *ṣwḥh* (v. 11) appears only four other times in the Hebrew Bible. Isa. 42.11 is an expression of joy. Jer. 46.12 refers to Egypt's cry of anguish. Ps. 144.14 is strikingly similar to our passage: 'May there be no more cry of distress in our streets'. Note also Jer. 14.2: 'and the cry

of Jerusalem goes up'. This lexical study presses the conclusion that the tone of lament in 24.4-12 is genuine, rather than simply a foil for the rejoicing in vv. 14-16a.

(3) Lindblom's view which builds on the jubilant nature of vv. 14-16a fails to consider the censorious tone expressed by the prophet in vv. 16bff. Plöger's conclusion supports my own: 'That the psalm of lament became a lampoon on the lips of the Jews . . . may be true in other cases, but finds no support in the present text'.[30]

Considerations such as the ones we have just mentioned led W.E. March to conclude that this section was patterned after the communal lament *Gattung*, as was noted above. While the tone, mood, and vocabulary support such a designation, I am hesitant to refer to this as a formal lament because so many of the elements of a lament are not present. According to C. Westermann there are three subjects present in the communal lament: (1) Thou, God; (2) we; (3) the enemy.[31] Since none of the three are mentioned here, it seems prudent not to define these verses formally in this way.[32]

The mood of lament is found in other *Gattungen* besides the lament proper. It is known particularly in the dirge. Occasionally, as O. Eissfeldt has noted, prophets will 'politicize' a funeral dirge and apply it 'to the "death" of communities' and cities.[33] The funeral dirge is preeminently politicized in Lamentations 1, 2 and 4 where the tone and vocabulary are reminiscent of Isaiah 24. The fact that the introductory word (*'ykh*) is missing in ch. 24 shows only that the prophet felt free to modify this form for his own purposes. Amos also altered the form when he took 'an already existing "non-prophetic" political dirge',[34] and put it to prophetic use:

> Fallen, no more to rise, is the virgin Israel;
> Prostrate on her land, with none to raise her up (5.2).

Because Isa. 24.7-12 describes the 'death' of a city, and does so in the vocabulary of a lament, we conclude that the *Gattung* is that of a political dirge.

4. *A Prophetic Reinterpretation*

It is particularly striking that the concluding phrase in 24.3, *ky yhwy dbr . . .*, did not refer to any word spoken by Yahweh in the first person. Undoubtedly, it refers to the prophetic word in vv. 1-3a as a word from Yahweh. But whose prophetic word might this be? W.L. Holladay has suggested that it is a word from Isaiah of Jerusalem which was originally directed against the land of Judah; it was an allusion to an 'earthquake experienced or envisioned ("he will twist its surface", v. 1)'.[35] His reasoning for assigning this announcement to First Isaiah is twofold: (1) Similarity of style: the list of opposites in v. 2 corresponds to the lists in 3.2-3; 2.13-16; 10.9; 11.6-7, and (2) Isaiah prophesied again and again against the land (*'rṣ* = land or earth) of Judah (cf. 1.7; 6.12, etc.).[36]

This is an attractive proposal and I would add four additional items of support: (1) H. Wildberger has noted that the syntactical arrangement of *hnh* followed by Yahweh as subject plus a participle occurs frequently in First Isaiah (3.1; 8.7; 10.33; 19.1; 22.17), while elsewhere in the OT it occurs only rarely.[37] It may be objected that the author of Isa. 24–27 simply was imitating a stylistic feature of First Isaiah, though, in light of recent studies by R. Polzin and A. Hurvitz, such imitation of style appears unlikely.[38] (2) G.B. Gray has indirectly supported Holladay's view by suggesting that *'rṣ* originally may have meant 'land', 'for if the whole earth is emptied, whither are the inhabitants dispersed?'[39] (3) The vocabulary used to describe the devastation of the earth in vv. 1-3 is different from that in vv. 4ff., which may suggest that vv. 1-3 originated with a different author. (4) The word, *bzz* (v. 3), was important in Isaiah's pronouncements of judgment. In 8.1, 3 its nominative form becomes part of his son's name which symbolized the judgment which was to come upon Samaria and Damascus (*mhr šll hš bz*). In 10.6 the infinitive form is used in reference to Assyria's attack on Israel.

We also note that this first unit (vv. 1-13) concludes by employing the language of First Isaiah (v. 13b = 17.6). Further, the phrase, *bqrb h'rṣ*, as the location of Yahweh's judgment is frequently used by Isaiah (5.8; 6.12; 10.23).

This analysis has shown that both the opening and closing portions of this unit are futuristic and 'Isaianic'. They form a bracket around the description of devastation in vv. 4-12. The fact that the author intentionally bracketed the description of destruction with earlier, Isaianic predictions of judgment strongly suggests that he viewed these events which he is describing as the fulfillment of earlier Isaianic prophecy. In my judgment, the author of Isa. 24–27 was continuing the prophetic tradition of reinterpretation, the genius of which was its affirmation that the prophetic word was not exhausted in the lifetime of the prophet who uttered it, but was to be used to interpret later events in the life of the community.[40] We know that the earlier oracles applied to the events of 732-722 and 701 BCE. It is our view that the events of 587 BCE are now being interpreted in light of these earlier oracles of Isaiah. It would be an obvious step for an observer of the destruction of Jerusalem at the hands of the Babylonians to apply to this situation the prophetic word of the prophet whose calling it was to proclaim to Israel and Judah their doom (6.1-12). In an effort to interpret the catastrophic events of his day this author sought the help of the prophecies of Isaiah.

Of course this view rests on the supposition that vv. 4-12 refer to the destruction of Jerusalem. Since very few interpreters subscribe to this position, it will require extensive substantiation. To this task we now turn our attention.

5. *The Focus of 24.1-13*

In the history of interpretation of this unit, there have been two dominant views. (1) The present *communis opinio* is that vv. 1-13 depict a worldwide destruction. According to this position, *'rṣ* is to be translated, 'earthy', the everlasting covenant, *bryt 'wlm*, is a reference to the Noachic covenant, and the destroyed city is either a foreign city identical with the city mentioned in 25.2; 26.5, 6; 27.10, or a representative city whose destruction illustrates the termination of city life in general. It is further maintained that this portrayal of universal destruction introduces onto the pages of the OT a nascent apocalypticism.[41] (2) On the other hand, a minority of scholars have argued that the destruction is focused on the land of Judah, that the *bryt 'wlm* refers to the Mosaic covenant, and the city which is reduced to chaos is Jerusalem. My own analysis has led me to a conclusion that is closely related to the second position: The language is cosmic but it is focused on the country of Judah, the covenant is the Mosaic covenant, and the city is Jerusalem. The following study will concentrate on these three central points: (a) the meaning of *'rṣ*; (b) the nature of the *bryt 'wlm*; (c) the identity of the city.

(a) *The Meaning of* 'rṣ

Gesenius, R. Lowth, R. Smend, and R.B.Y. Scott[42] each translated *'rṣ* as 'land' throughout the first thirteen verses. As to the troublesome parallelism between *'rṣ* and *tbl* in v. 4, Gesenius insisted that 'Welt steht für das Reich, wie 13.11 und 26.9'.[43] Lowth maintained that 'the world is the same with land; that is, the kingdom of Judah and

Israel; *orbis Israeliticus*'.[44] Smend held that the parallelism was controlled by *'rṣ* rather than by *tbl*.[45] Finally, Scott saw the parallelism as 'extended' rather than synonymous: 'not only the land but the whole world'.[46]

In my view, none of these arguments is convincing. (1) Gesenius referred to Isa. 13.11 and 26.9 as examples of *tbl* indicating a specific kingdom or realm. But Isa. 13.1-16 is a general statement about the destructive activity of Yahweh, employing typical theophanic language. It describes the destruction of the cosmic realm. Only with v. 17 does the destruction begin to focus on a particular people. The introductory *hnny* and the naming of specific nations for the first time strongly suggest that vv. 17ff. were originally a separate unit which has been joined to a section which portrays the day of Yahweh in graphic and general terminology.[47]

In 26.9 the author is using stereotypical language to contrast the righteous and the wicked. The 'inhabitants of the world' refer to non-Israelites, though the context redirects the phrase so that it is made to refer specifically to the oppressor of Judah. The phrase becomes an epithet, but within the phrase, *tbl* still means 'world'.

(2) Smend maintained that *'rṣ* controlled the parallelism and that *tbl* did not necessarily mean the entire earth.[48] But this reasoning appears forced to me. It must be recognized that the normal understanding of *tbl* is cosmic in nature.

(3) Finally, it is difficult to see why Scott's proposal of 'extended' rather than 'synonymous' parallelism does anything but argue against his own position. He even acknowledges that 'the whole world' is included.

While I have maintained that *'rṣ* must be translated as 'earth', I do not thereby conclude that the focus of these verses is a universal, worldwide catastrophe. Gesenius and the others failed to recognize that the language was indeed cosmic in nature, but they were correct in seeing its focus as national. This is the position of E.J. Kissane and W.E. March, who suggest that *'rṣ*, while it should be translated 'earth', should be taken in a 'figurative', non-literal sense, rather than in a geographical sense.[49]

We know that theophanic language is characterized by hyperbolic imagery. We know further that often in the OT cosmic language is employed even though the judgment is restricted to a particular nation.[50] In light of this, one must consider other factors before deciding whether the cosmic language refers to a universal or local situation.

(b) *The Nature of the* bryt ʿwlm

Those who understand vv. 1-13 as portraying a universal destruction regard the *bryt ʾwlm* as the Noachic covenant which all humankind has broken. But the overwhelming weight of the evidence supports the fact that the covenant in question is the Mosaic covenant.

(1) The phrase, *bryt ʿwlm*, occurs in conjunction with other terms that are suggestive of the Mosaic covenant: *twrh*, *ḥq*.[51] In my reconstruction of the Hebrew text (see Appendix), I suggest that the original text read *twrh* (singular) rather than *twrt*. If I am correct then the Mosiac reference is unmistakable. If the original text read *twrt*, then the allusion to the Mosaic covenant is still hardly to be doubted since *twrt* is never used with reference to any group of people other than the covenant people.[52] The same is true of the term *ḥq*.[53]

(2) The context in which the phrase *bryt ʿwlm* occurs is that of a covenant law-suit. Such an association would seem inappropriate in a universal setting. Yahweh consistently judges the nations because of their hubris, not because they have broken a covenant (cf. the oracles against the nations, especially Isa. 13.11; 14.13; 16.6; also 10.12-19; 37.21-29; 47; also, the oracles against the nations in Jer. 46–51. Note that Amos, with all his reasons for denouncing the nations, does not once refer to transgression of the law; this he reserves for the people of Judah—chs. 1 and 2).

(3) Even though the Mosaic/sinaitic covenant is never elsewhere referred to as a *bryt ʿwlm*, it is associated with the term *ʿwlm* on at least three occasions:

a. Judg. 2.1	*lʾ ʾpr bryt ʾtkm lʿwlm*
b. Ps. 111.5, 9	*yzkr lʿwlm brytw*
	ṣwḥ-lʿwlm brytw
c. Exod. 31.16	The sabbath which is a sign of the Mosaic covenant is known as a *bryt ʿwlm*.[54]

(4) If we are correct in suggesting that the author of Isa. 24–27 was making a conscious attempt to link his prophetic word with the oracles of First Isaiah, then we might legitimately look to Isa. 33.8 as the antecedent for this covenant motif. This is the only other mention of covenant in First Isaiah (except 28.15—a 'covenant with death'). The context of devastation and mourning is similarly connected with a breach of covenant.[55]

(5) It was impossible for humanity to break the Noachic covenant. It was simply a promise by God never again to destroy the world by a

flood. There is no mention of human responsibility, nor even of human involvement in this covenant. Gerhard von Rad characteristically has expressed this point with significant force:

> This covenant with Noah differs from that with Abraham, the covenant on Sinai and all other covenants in that in the latter instances the individual or nation was called quite personally into a relation of fellowship with God and thereby faced with the question of affirming this ordinance. Here the sign of the covenant with Noah, absolutely without any confessing appropriation by the earthly partner, is high above man, between heaven and earth, as pledge of a true *gratia praeveniens* (grace coming before the will)![56]

The problem is aggravated by the fact that the construction *hprw bryt 'wlm* is oxymoronic in nature. An everlasting covenant by definition cannot be broken. Unless we assume that the author has created a nonsensical construction, we must conclude that he intended the Mosaic covenant which both could be broken, and was described on various occasions as being *'wlm*.

It must also be recognized that the idea of judgment against all humanity because of their unfaithfulness to the Noachic covenant is without parallel in the OT.

Similarly, I know of no other occurrence in the OT of the motif of the total destruction of the present age; the universal devastation of heaven and earth. Von Rad refers to 'several of apocalyptic literature's perspectives of the absolute end of the whole present existence of heaven and earth', but the passage he cites is Isa. 24.17-23![57] This is a later, intertestamental theme. Its occurrence in the sixth century would be without parallel. Rather, what we have in the OT is the use of theophanic, 'Day of Yahweh' language in which cosmic language is ubiquitous. But this is applied consistently to specific nations rather than to the termination of the present age.

The closest the OT comes to a description of the end of the present age is in Jer. 4.23-28, which depicts a return to chaos. But this is Jeremiah's way of describing the destruction of Jerusalem and the ensuing exile which he perceived as imminent. Again, this is an example of cosmic imagery applied to a specific geographical situation.

Finally, it is commonly asserted that the reference to the pollution of the land, *wh'rṣ ḥnph* (v. 5), is an indirect allusion to the Noachic covenant, since in Num. 35.33 it is stated that blood that is shed on the land will pollute that land, and the shedding of blood was one of the things forbidden to Noah, and through him, to all humanity—Gen. 9.1-7.

In my view it is highly problematic to base a claim for the Noachic covenant on the reference to the pollution of the land in v. 5 for two reasons: (1) In the Genesis account the law against bloodshed and the covenant promise which God made to Noah are in two distinct and separate pericopae. The one is in no way contingent on the other.[58] (2) The context for the passage in Num. 35.33 makes it clear that the prohibition against pollution is because of Yahweh's ownership of the land:

> You shall not defile the land in which you live, in the midst of which I dwell; for I the Lord dwell in the midst of the people of Israel (Num. 35.34).

It is therefore highly unlikely that this pericope could have been an antecedent in the history of tradition for the notion of the pollution of the whole earth. The religious context of 24.5 suggests instead a tradition similar to that of Jer. 3.2, 9 and Ps. 106.38 where idolatry and religious harlotry are the cause of the pollution of the land.

(c) *The Identity of the City*

Scholars have generally identified the city of 24.10 either (1) with the cities of 25.2; 26.5, 6; 27.10[59] or (2) as a representative city, a 'vanity fair'.[60] However, the following six considerations have led me to conclude that the city is Jerusalem:

(1) The *Gattung* of 24.7-12. I noted above (p. 23) that the tone and mood were those of a lament, and I suggested that the prophet had employed the funeral dirge in a politicized fashion to describe the death of the city. It is doubtful that the author would mourn the destruction of an enemy city. Indeed, a comparison with 25.1-5, a hymn of praise, and 26.1-6, a victory song, both of which anticipate the destruction of an (oppressive) enemy city only highlights the lament-like tone of 24.7-12, and makes it impossible to equate the city of 24.10 with the city of 25.2 and 26.5, 6.[61]

While it is reasonable to assume that the author was not referring to the foreign city mentioned elsewhere in the composition, may we therefore conclude that he was referring to his own city, Jerusalem? Of course those interpreters who view these verses as a depiction of worldwide devastation would demur. O. Plöger maintains that the author is referring to 'the city life of contemporary civilization in general, which Yahweh's destructive activity will not by-pass'.[62] H. Wildberger's position varies only slightly from this. He thinks that the concrete, descriptive details argue for a particular city, however, that city, he maintains, now functions as a representative city, the downfall of which signals the coming of the end.[63]

I must object to Plöger's view because there is nothing in the text that would suggest that 'city life in general' is the primary focus. As Wildberger has so ably noted, the focus is on a specific city. And one must ask of Wildberger what city other than Jerusalem could possibly function in such a representative way. Only the destruction of Jerusalem, the dwelling place of Yahweh, could cause a Jewish author to envision the return to chaos that he sketches in vv. 18-20.

(2) The phrase *mśwś h'rṣ*. Any case for identifying the city in 24.10 with Jerusalem which rests on *Gattung* alone must be inconclusive. What that has shown is (1) that this city is not to be identified with the city (or cities) of 25.2 and 26.5, 6, and (b) that in all probability the city is one which the author viewed with deep appreciation. But more is needed to identify the city with Jerusalem. In my view, the phrase *mśwś h'rṣ* carries an intentional *double entendre* which supports such an identification. It is used in parallel with *'rbh kl śmḥh* to indicate a cessation of joy. But it also functions as an epithet for Jerusalem. This expression occurs as a descriptive phrase for Jerusalem in Lam. 2.15:

> Is this the city which was called, 'the perfection of beauty', 'the joy of all the earth' (*mśwś kl h'rṣ*)?

It has the same function in Ps. 48.3:

> Beautiful in elevation is the joy of all the earth, Mt Zion is the heights of Zaphon, the city of the great king.

The use of the verb *glh* in connection with this phrase supports our position, for in the prophetic literature *glh* consistently carries the connotation of going into exile.[64] This is true of First Isaiah as the reference in 5.13 indicates:

> Therefore my people go into exile for want of knowledge;
> their honored men are dying of hunger,
> and their multitude is parched with thirst.[65]

In light of the numerous other points of contact with Isaiah 5 throughout chs. 24–27,[66] one might assume an interrelationship at this point. I conclude that to any reader in the Isaianic tradition, the *double entendre* would have been self-evident.

W. Rudolph is one of the few interpreters who have seen this allusion to Jerusalem. But because he had already determined that the unit dealt with a worldwide catastrophe, and that the city was a foreign city, he eliminated the phrase as a secondary gloss.[67]

H. Wildberger fails to see the epithetic nature of this phrase. Rather he suggests that the author of the 'addition' (vv. 10-12) used the phrase to connect the destruction of the city with the worldwide catastrophe.[68] But such a view suggests a disjointed thought pattern: from the city (10-11b) to the earth (11c), and back to the city (12). But if the phrase, *mśwś h'rṣ*, is seen as an epithet for the city, then the entire pericope focuses on the city. One suspects that Wildberger's assumption about the universal focus of this material has prevented him from seeing the special nuances that the author undoubtedly intended.

(3) The similarity between 5.11-14 and 24.8, 9 is so striking that it is possible to perceive an exegetical relationship between the two pericopae. In addition to the repetition of vocabulary (*tpym/tp, knwr, yyn, škr*) the ideas of revelry and rejoicing are common to both. Isaiah had prophesied against those who did not regard the deeds of Yahweh, who were so single-minded in their merry-making that they lived only for themselves (5.11). They would therefore be taken into exile (5.13, 14). The author of chs. 24–27 saw in the events which were transpiring the fulfillment of this earlier prophecy. The wine and beer with which they used to begin and end their day have been taken away. The situation is as Isaiah had prophesied: 'their multitude is parched with thirst' (5.13). The instruments which had provided the backdrop for their revelry are now silent. The city is destroyed (cf. 5.17). Finally, Isaiah had announced that 'her throng (*šwnh*) and he who exults (*'lz*) in her' would be destroyed (5.14). In 24.8 the author observes that the *šwn 'lyzym*, 'noise of the revelers' has ceased.[69]

(4) There are several scholars who see the phrase, *bqrb h'rṣ* (v. 13), as an allusion to Jerusalem as the 'center of the earth'. J. Lindblom is one who holds this view:

> Die 'Mitte der Erde' bedeutet hier Judaea, das Land der jüdischen Gemeinde. Es ist in der nachexilischen Zeit ein sehr gewöhnlicher Gedanke, daß das kleine Juda wie in einer Oase mitten in der Völkerwüste lebte. Jerusalem mit seinem Tempel und seiner

> Gemeinde bildete den Nabel der Erde, und die Juden saßen gleichsam in der Mitte mit den Heidenvölkern ringsherum.[70]

But because he failed to see the earlier allusions to Jerusalem, and because he insisted that 24.10 was a reference to Babylon, he found the transition from vv. 1-12 to v. 13 to be strained: 'Es muß allerdings zugestanden werden, daß im Text die Gedankenverbindung zwischen v. 12 and v. 13 nicht unmittelbar deutlich ist'.[71] But the problem is not in the lack of clarity in the text, but rather in Lindblom's misunderstanding of the focus of vv. 7-12. There is no problem of transition when the city is identified as Jerusalem.

P.L. Redditt also argues that *bqrb h'rṣ* suggests the city of Jerusalem. From the work of A.J. Wensinck (*The Ideas of Western Semites Concerning the Navel of the Earth*) he lists several characteristics of the navel of the earth:

1. It is elevated above the surrounding territory.
2. It is the origin of the earth, as the navel is the origin of the embryo.
3. It lies at the center of the earth.
4. It is the place of communion with nether and upper worlds.
5. It is the medium by which food is distributed over the earth.[72]

He concludes that since Jerusalem fits this description, then the phrase *bqrb h'rṣ* is to be understood as a reference to Jerusalem.

While Redditt's analysis may support the identification of the city as Jerusalem, there is a serious methodological problem which prevents it from being conclusive on its own merit. The issue is not whether 'navel of the earth' imagery is applicable to Jerusalem—certainly it is—but whether the phrase *bqrb h'rṣ* in its present setting is intended to convey the notion of the 'navel of the earth'.

In my judgment the phrase *bqrb h'rṣ may* function as a reference to Jerusalem as 'the center of the earth',[73] but not necessarily so. When the phrase occurs in Isa. 5.8; 6.12; 7.22 the context suggests the reading, 'throughout the land', though the implication is clear that Jerusalem/Judah are the focus.

The parallel phrase, *btwk h'mym*, is similarly ambiguous. Wildberger uses it to defend this reading of *bqrb h'rṣ* in the broadest possible sense: both phrases refer to the entire world.[74] But such a conclusion is not imperative. One has only to note the similar reference in Ezek. 5.5:

> Thus says Yahweh, 'This is Jerusalem; I have set her in the center of the nations (*btwk hgwym*)'.

The phrase *btwk hgwym* is parallel to *btwk h'mym*, which suggests that the latter could also refer to Jerusalem as the midpoint of the peoples of the world.

Dogmatism regarding the proper understanding of *bqrb h'rṣ//btwk h'mym* is to be avoided. The identity of Jerusalem certainly could never rest on these expressions alone. But given the fact that (a) Jerusalem is pictured as the center of the earth in Isa. 2.2 (and also designated later in *Jub*. 8.19 and *Enoch* 26.1ff.) and increasingly took on this connotation in the exilic and post-exilic times, and (b) there are several other allusions to Jerusalem in this pericope, I conclude that *bqrb h 'rṣ* is another case of *double entendre*: the destruction is portrayed in cosmic terms, but the focus is on Jerusalem, the city which stands at the center of the earth, in the midst of the peoples.

(5) Vocabulary.[75] The terms *'bl* and *'mll* are employed frequently in connection with the destructive activity of Yahweh. As ubiquitous as these words are, then, it is striking that in the prophetic literature, in every case but two (Isa. 16.8; 19.8) the reference is to the land or people of Israel/Judah. Note the following:

> And her (Jerusalem's) gates shall lament and mourn;
> ravaged, she shall sit upon the ground (Isa. 3.26).
>
> The land (of Israel) mourns and languishes (Isa. 33.9).

An interesting 'twist' occurs in Third Isaiah, for here the references speak of turning the mourning (*'bl*) into joy and gladness (cf. 57.18; 60.20; 61.2, 3; 66.10). In all these references it is Zion which has been in a state of mourning similar to what we have presented in 24.4-12.

A glance at Jeremiah, Hosea, Amos, and particularly Lamentations[76] reveals several passages which parallel Isa. 24.4-12. Note particularly: (a) Hos. 4.1-3. The prophet announces that Yahweh is engaged in a covenant law-suit with his people because of their unfaithfulness. The result is the 'mourning' and 'languishing' of both land and people; (b) Amos 8.8. Because of Israel's sins its inhabitants will mourn. This confirms our suspicion that the prophets generally reserved this terminology for the suffering of their own land and people. When they depicted the judgment of Yahweh on foreign nations, for the most part, they drew upon other terminology.

The term *nbl* occurs in First Isaiah three times: 1.30; 28.1, and 4—in oracles of judgment against Israel/Judah.[77] If the claim for prophetic reinterpretation of Isaianic oracles can be sustained, then the choise of *nbl* is understandable.

The verb *'nḥ* (always in Niphal), appears twelve times in the OT. Except for the general reference in Prov. 29.2 and the reference to beasts in Joel 1.18, this term is applied solely to the people of Yahweh. Note particularly Lam. 1.4, 8, 11, 21, in which the similarity to Isaiah 24 is striking.[78] Once again, the anguish of other nations is expressed consistently with other terms.

Finally, we cite the term *šmh*—v. 12, and related passages in First Isaiah:

> Your country lies desolate,
> your cities are burned with fire;
> in your very presence aliens devour your land;
> it is desolate, as overthrown by aliens (Isa. 1.7).

In response to Isaiah's query at his commissioning, 'How long, O Lord?' Yahweh answered:

> Until cities lie waste without inhabitant,
> and houses without men,
> and the land is utterly desolate (Isa. 6.11).
> Surely many houses will be desolate (Isa. 5.9b).

This discussion of the vocabulary employed by the author of 24.4-12 suggests two things: First, the fact that he chose terms which, within the prophetic tradition, were commonly used with reference to the devastation of Israel/Judah rather than the demise of the foreign nations lends support to our thesis that vv. 4-12 refer to the destruction of Jerusalem rather than to a foreign city or to the whole world. Second, the fact that this author, in describing the destruction of a land and city, draws heavily upon the same terms which First Isaiah had used to prophesy against Judah, suggests (especially in light of our discussion of the function of vv. 1-3 and 13) that he saw the events of his day as the fulfillment of Isaiah's prophecy.

Related to the category of vocabulary is a consideration of the term *mrwm*—v. 4. Throughout the prophetic literature and the Psalms, this term is closely associated with Mt Zion, the dwelling place of Yahweh. Note the following:

> Yahweh is exalted, for he dwells on high (*mrwm*);
> he will fill Zion with justice and righteousness (Isa. 33.5).

The parallelism identifies *mrwm* with Mt Zion.

> Why look you with envy, O many-peaked mountain,
> at the mount which God desired for his abode,
> yea, where Yahweh will dwell for ever? . . .
> You (Yahweh) have gone up to the height (*mrwm*) (Ps. 68.17, 19; author's trans.).

Once again, the identification of *mrwm* and Mt Zion is self-evident.[79] I refer finally to a passage from Jeremiah:

> A glorious throne on high (*mrwm*) from the beginning is the place of our sanctuary (Jer. 17.12).[80]

These references suggest a certain correspondence between the term, *mrwm*, and Mt Zion. Of course, no one would argue that every occurrence of *mrwm* was an allusion to Mt Zion as Isa. 26.5 readily shows. However, the phrase, 'the high place of the earth' seems an unnecessary addition to v. 4 if there is not a particular connotation implied. In this verse, the *'rṣ* and *tbl* already convey the meaning of an all-encompassing scope. For some reason the author wanted to focus on the 'high place' of the earth. In the light of the Isaianic tradition which proclaimed Jerusalem as the apogee of the entire earth (Isa. 2.2), it is difficult to imagine any other locale which would be referred to as 'the high place of the earth'. And because of the other references to Jerusalem within this unit, one may assume a similar allusion to it here (see p. 42 for comment on *mrwm* in v. 18b).

(6) I mention one final factor which suggests that the focus of the destruction was on Jerusalem: the response of the prophet in v. 16b to the rejoicing of the Jews.[81] If the people of Judah were to be circumvented by the judgment, then it is difficult to understand the prophet's agonized cry, *w'mr rzy-ly rzy-ly 'wy ly*. Later, when he considers the destruction of the foreign city, he is unable to contain his feelings of praise and joy (25.1-5; 26.1-6). But when similar feelings are expressed in vv. 14-16a as a response to the events described in vv. 1-13, the prophet replies in acrimonious fashion.

B. *An Inappropriate Response (24.14-16aα)*

Commentators are in general agreement about the termination of this pericope at v. 16aα primarily because of the climax reached at *ṣby lṣdyq* and the contrastive note that is struck with *w'mr* in v. 16aβ.[82] It is also agreed that this is a hymn of praise. But there is little accord regarding either the identity of the *hmh* or the function of the pericope in its present context. The troublesome nature of these few verses is well summarized by G.B. Gray: 'no complete and satisfactory interpretation of them (14-16a) in their present position seems possible'.[83] And a survey of the several attempts at interpretation lends support to Gray's statement. What is needed is a fresh approach.

1. *The Identity of the* hmh

Most interpreters follow Rudolph in rejecting the notion that *hmh* refers to 'non-Jews' or 'heathen', primarily because the language and ascription of praise to Yahweh is inappropriate for the heathen, or at the least would have required some indication of their having turned to Yahweh.[84] Only Gray seriously entertains the idea that this hymn could be a confession by Gentiles. For support he suggests that 17.6 which is the original oracle on which v. 13 is based 'is immediately followed (17.7) by a statement that all mankind will turn "to the Holy One of Israel"'.[85] But it is doubtful that simply because the term *h'dm* is used in 17.7 one can demonstrate that all humankind is referred to; rather, Isaiah continues to speak of the people of Samaria. We must conclude, with the majority of scholars, that those who break forth in hymnic praise are Jews.

At the same time we must recognize the force of another of Gray's arguments, namely, that the connection between vv. 14ff. and the preceding is such that *hmh* 'must be explained by what precedes'.[86] This is true despite the fact that vv. 14-16a may have been an independent unit at one time, for it is clear that in their present setting they are viewed as the continuation of vv. 1-13.

Rudolph, Procksch, and Wildberger understand *hmh* as a reference to the Jews of the Diaspora.[87] On the surface this is an attractive proposal because the hymn is reminiscent of Isa. 42.10-12, a hymn of the exiles. Further, the geographical points might suggest the diaspora. However, as our translation indicates, the call to praise does not originate from the four points of the earth, but is directed to them. Further, it is to be recognized that it is a common feature of such hymns of praise to appeal to the far reaches of the earth and the sea without regard for a particular people (cf. Pss. 98.1-3; 117). This is certainly true of Isa. 42.10-12, as the phrase, 'let the sea roar and all that fills it' indicates. In both this pericope and Isa. 24.14-16aα all peoples are being summoned to praise Yahweh, but they are being summoned by Jews.

The most serious objection to the view espoused by these interpreters is that the sudden appearance of diaspora Jews in vv. 14-16a would destroy any connection between vv. 14-16a and the preceding verses, because by their own account, these interpreters see no allusion to diaspora Judaism in vv. 1-13. The result is that *hmh* has no antecedent.

Lindblom, on the other hand, is careful to maintain a close connection between vv. 14-16aα and the preceding verses. Because he understands v. 13 as a reference to the 'navel of the earth' (Jerusalem), he thinks that *hmh* must refer to the Jews of Palestine who will escape the judgment.[88]

Lindblom's view presumes that the purpose of v. 13 is to highlight the existence of a remnant. But in my view, this is not the purpose of v. 13. Its primary theme is judgment. It summarizes all that has gone before in such a manner that it also indicates the pervasiveness of the judgment. To be sure, v. 13 is modeled on 17.6, which speaks both of judgment and a remnant (*š'r*). But it is important to note that any notion of *š'r* is left out of 24.13, which speaks only of the 'beating of the olive tree', and 'gleaning' which takes place after the initial harvest is finished.

This interpretation of *k'wllt* is supported by its parallelism with *knqp*: like the beating // like the gleaning (contra BDB, p. 760, which insists that *'wllt* always refers to a remnant; cf. Judg. 8.2; 20.45; Mic. 7.1). If a remnant is alluded to at all, it is only an incidental allusion. Therefore it is unlikely that *hmh* refers to 'the remnant' in v. 13.

Ultimately the determination of the identity of *hmh* must relate itself to the function of the pericope. To that we now turn our attention.

2. *The Function of vv. 14-16aα*

The key to interpreting this pericope is found in the note of contrast between the people's hymn of praise and the prophet's cry of woe in the line that follows. His tone is one of reprimand and rebuke. Clearly he views their words as inappropriate in the situation.

In my view, this element of contrast is either denied or downplayed by most interpreters. Lindblom negates the contrast by severing any relationship between v. 16aβ and the preceding lines: 'Mit v. 16aβ beginnt ein Gedicht mit ganz neuem Inhalt . . . 16aβ-20 muß also als ein selbständiges Gedicht behandelt werden'. He then facilitates this view by dismissing *w'mr* as a redactional linkword.[89] But few scholars have been convinced by this argument. As Duhm and then Marti have indicated, the rhyme between *ṣby* and *rzy* is intentional: 'Not *ṣ*ᵉ*bî* but *rāzî* for me', cries the prophet.[90] The connection would be lost on Lindblom's view.[91]

Millar regards vv. 14-16aα as a completely appropriate response of joy:

> In the face of all the terror to accompany Yahweh's march in New Conquest, there were still grounds for rejoicing. Evil was having its last stand. Yahweh, the Divine Warrior, would be victorious and stand again as King (Is. 24.23).[92]

But if Millar's view is correct then the prophet has completely missed the reason for jubilation. His cry of woe makes no sense.

Wildberger seems unclear on this matter. On the one hand he implies that the prophet is distraught at the people's rejoicing because he believes that the judgment will not circumvent them, and they are not aware of it.[93] Later he suggests that this hymn originated within a particular circle of diaspora Jews who failed to realize the seriousness of the destruction of the earth. However, he fails to indicate whether the prophet believed these same Jews would be included in the destruction.[94]

Plöger takes a rather presumptuous approach to this difficult problem:

> The point of the objection should be evident: the author is protesting against the superficial view, which expresses itself in premature joy as a result of preliminary, pre-eschatological events and thus detracts from the eschatological activity of Yahweh.[95]

But a simply superficial view would doubtless not warrant the intensity of the prophet's *Angstruf* in response. He reacts so strongly because the people have missed his point so completely. Not only will they not escape the judgment, but it is directed specifically against them.

I noted above that in vv. 1-13 the prophet predicted the imminent destruction of Jerusalem. I noted further that the *hmh* must be defined by its antecedent in the preceding verses, and that in light of the hymn of praise which followed, *hmh* must refer to Jews. This was troublesome for most interpreters because they failed to see that the people of Judah/Jerusalem were the focus of vv. 1-13.

Given this observation, there are two possible explanations for the people's reaction of praise. (1) It may be that the prophet, writing in the tradition of the one who created the parable of the vineyard (5.1-7), employed obscure imagery of his own in order to trap his hearers. They think that the judgment is directed against their enemies, but the prophet responds with, 'Panic and pit and pitfall are upon you!' As we have observed above, even those interpreters who view vv. 1-13 as depicting a worldwide catastrophe recognize that the prophet believes that his fellow Jews will not escape the destruction. Either way, they have misunderstood the seriousness of the judgment.

(2) I suggest another view which takes more seriously the historical context of the period. If we take our cue from the note of contrast that is evidenced in these verses, then we find something of a parallel in Isaiah 22. Note the comment by Gray regarding ch. 22:

> Clear and insistent in this section is the contrast between the prophet's dark vision of destruction and the light-heartedness and recklessness of the people, who . . . do not perceive the issue of things.[96]

With the sudden departure of Sennacherib from his siege of Jerusalem the populace of the city took to the rooftops with expressions of joy at their miraculous deliverance. But Isaiah rebuked them, delivering an oracle of judgment (vv. 12-14). Later, during the fateful days of 597-587 this oracle was employed to shed light on this most recent attack of Jerusalem.[97] We may imagine that there were those who continued to hold to the inviolability of Zion and rejoiced at Nebuchadnezzar's departure, seeing it as a parallel to Sennacherib's departure, and again giving praise to Yahweh for sparing the city. For even though he had taken a heavy toll on the city (2 Kgs 24.10-17), he nevertheless left the city standing. But the perceptive prophet knew that this was only a temporary reprieve and that the 'Day of Yahweh' would surely come upon Jerusalem (v. 5).

It is clear from the book of Jeremiah that optimism regarding the fate of Jerusalem remained strong even to the final hour. In Jer. 21.2 we read that King Zedekiah sent Pashhur and Zephaniah to Jeremiah with this message:

> Inquire of the Lord for us, for Nebuchadrezzar king of Babylon is making war against us; perhaps the Lord will deal with us according to all his wonderful deeds, and will make him withdraw from us.

The theory of the inviolability of Zion maintained its durability to the end as well.

> Do not trust in these deceptive words: This is the temple of the Lord, the temple of the Lord, the temple of the Lord (Jer. 7.4)

We know that after 597 it seemed to many observers that Yahweh's judgment had achieved its end and hopes for an imminent return were intense. In Jeremiah 27 we note these words of the prophet:

> Do not listen to the words of the prophets who are saying to you, 'You shall not serve the king of Babylon', for it is a lie which they are prophesying to you (27.14).

Again Jeremiah says:

> Thus says the Lord: Do not listen to the words of your prophets who are prophesying to you, saying, 'Behold, the vessels of the Lord's house will now shortly be brought back from Babylon', for it is a lie which they are prophesying to you (27.16).

If I am correct in my understanding of 24.1-13, that it is a prophecy of the imminent destruction of Jerusalem, then it follows that we should look to this historical situation for the circumstances which produced the hymn of praise in vv. 14–16aα. We may imagine that in v. 16a the prophet was responding to those Jews who, despite his prophecy of the total destruction of their city (24.20-22), upon seeing Nebuchadnezzar leave the city after 597, sing praise to Yahweh because he has again spared their city and left them as the surviving remnant. But the prophet, as Isaiah before him (22.5), announces that the Day of Yahweh is coming, from which they will find it impossible to escape (v. 17).

The advantages of this understanding of the function of vv. 14–16 are five-fold:

1. It recognizes that the antecedent to *hmh* is to be found in vv. 1-13. 'They' are the same people against whom Yahweh is moving in judgment, though they do not realize it.
2. This view recognizes that those who ascribe praise to Yahweh are Jews. But they do not appear 'out of nowhere', as it were, which is the problem with Wildberger's view.
3. This interpretation reflects the significant contrast that exists between the attitude of the people and that of the prophet.

4. This view is in concert with the other literature of the period which indicates a tension between the prophets who predicted destruction and those who proclaimed peace.
5. It will be observed that the prophet follows his exchange with the *hmh* with an announcement of judgment given in direct address: 'upon you'. The implication is that those people with whom he has been in dialogue, he now speaks to directly.[98] If such a shift is not assumed then any connection between vv. 16 and 17 is lost; v. 17 simply begins a new announcement of judgment.[99]

C. *The Announcement of Doom Continued (vv. 16aβ-20)*

Most interpreters agree that the unit ends with v. 20, with Rudolph as one of the few who extend the pericope to v. 23.[100] But the introductory formula, *whyh bywm hhw'* (v. 21), and the sudden change from *'rṣ* to *'dmh* argue against his position.

The phrase *'wy ly* is reminiscent of the cry of Isaiah during his call (6.5) and of Jeremiah at the realization of the tragic dimensions of the task he had been given (Jer. 10.19; 15.10). In both instances the prophets identify with their people and recognize that they stand under the judgment of Yahweh. We may assume that in the parallel passage in Isa. 24.16b the prophet also identifies with his people and realizes the inevitability of the judgment.[101]

In the text, the prophet's cry of woe is directly connected to the *bgdym*. Rudolph understood *bgdym*, 'the treacherous ones', as a reference to the prophet's own people, and thought there was an intended contrast between the *ṣdyq* and the *bgdym*. Rudolph concluded that the prophet believed that the sinfulness (treachery) of the people had necessitated the delay of the kingdom of God.[102] But there is nothing else in this passage which even hints at the notion of delay, so no one has followed Rudolph.

March, though he interprets the pericope differently than Rudolph, also views *bgdym* as a reference to the people of Judah. He argues that the term, *bgd*, can only refer to 'those who violate the covenant or prove unfaithful to Yahweh'.[103] According to this view, the subsequently described judgment (panic, pit and pitfall) comes because of the breach of covenant by the people of Judah. This would fit nicely with our view of 24.1-13, and even though March has compiled significant support for this understanding of *bgd* from elsewhere in the OT,[104] he has failed to note other occurrences of *bgd* such as Isa. 21.2; 33.1; 1.2, where the term refers to peoples other than the covenant people.

Wildberger thinks the writer is dependent on Isa. 21.2, though he admits that certainty is nearly impossible: 'Was *bgd* hier konkret meint, ist schwer zu sagen'.[105] To be sure, the similarity with 21.2 is striking. Most interpreters are in agreement that *hbwgd bwgd* (21.2) is a reference to the treachery of Babylon which Elam and Media are called upon to terminate.[106] This suggests that *bgdym* may have become an epithet for the Babylonians during the period of the late seventh and early sixth centuries. In that case the prophet in 24.16b cries in anguish because he knows that the Babylonians are not yet finished executing the judgment which Yahweh has given them.

Verses 17 and 18a are taken from Jer. 48.43 and reinterpreted so that they no longer refer to Moab, but to *ywšb h'rṣ*. Their function is to highlight the impossibility of escaping the impending doom.

Verse 18b suggests that the author is making a subtle allusion to the Ugaritic material in which Baal appears on his holy mountain with devastating power at the opening of the window of his new temple.[107] Similarly, Yahweh acts from his holy mountain (*mrwm*) in destroying the earth. The combined effect is an overwhelming sense that the creation is returning to chaos.[108] The prophet closes with a reference to Amos's dirge over fallen Israel (Amos 5.2), suggesting that just as Israel had succumbed to the weight of its transgressions, so now Judah would suffer a similar fate.

D. *Interpretation of 24.1-20*

1. *Unresolved Tensions*

Our analysis of 24.1-20 has revealed a striking combination of universalistic, cosmic imagery with language that suggests a special focus on a particular geographical location, viz. the center of the earth, Jerusalem. It is this merging of motifs that gives these verses their particular character. However, in the history of scholarship, interpreters have tended to view the data through only one perspective: the particular *or* the universal.

As we have seen, scholars such as Gesenius, Lowth, Scott, Kissane, and March have concentrated almost solely on those points which allude to Jerusalem and the covenant people. The cosmic imagery is simply discarded.

The second group of interpreters apply a contextual method of interpretation. They interpret the particular details of the text from the point of view of the greater context. In principle, such a methodology is entirely appropriate. But the practitioner must beware of flattening out the details to accommodate a supposed context when in fact the particular details may shed significant light on the meaning of the greater context.

On an interpretive level, some scholars deny that there are any allusions to a particular people. Having established that the context concerns the universal destruction of humanity, they then insist that the terms *twrh* and *ḥq*, which are normally associated with the Mosaic covenant, in this instance refer to the 'natural law' which is known to all human beings.[109] But Gesenius is correct in noting that such a view runs completely contrary to the Hebrew mind which knows no law except the revealed law.[110] Mandelkern's Concordance supports Gesenius, as *twrh* (or *twrt*) and *ḥq* are never employed elsewhere to substantiate the culpability of non-Israelites.[111]

Wildberger has recently taken an approach which he designates as 'Uminterpretation'. This tack is to be distinguished from that of earlier interpreters in that it does not force him to excise troublesome portions of the text, nor does it require him to deny what is clearly stated in the individual texts. Rather, he maintains that the author reinterprets material so that texts which originally referred to Israel are now construed in such a way that they refer to all humanity. For example, he recognizes that the evidence for the Mosaic/sinaitic covenant in v. 5 is undeniable.[112] But because the Mosaic covenant has been intentionally intertwined, *ineinandergeflossen*, with what Wildberger thinks is the Noachic covenant (*bryt 'wlm*, but see our discussion above), that which was originally directed toward Israel is now redirected toward humanity in general.[113] Likewise, the phrase, *mśwś h'rṣ*, no longer is nuanced to allude to Jerusalem, but is reinterpreted by its context to apply to the whole earth.[114]

That prophetic reinterpretation of earlier material occurs in the OT is not to be denied. We observed it in 24.1-3, 13, and also find it in 55.3, a passage in which the prophet of the exile has reinterpreted the covenant with David so that it is extended to the *people* of Israel. We noted, too, that 24.17, 18a is a reinterpretation of an oracle which, on another occasion, was directed against Moab (cf. Lam. 3.47). Finally, J.J.M. Roberts has shown convincingly that some of the prophecies of Isaiah which were initially directed against the northern kingdom were later redirected against Judah.[115]

In principle, then, it is certainly correct to appeal to the idea of reinterpretation when the text merits it. But one must not employ this notion in such a way that it distorts the intended meaning of the text. In my judgment, the allusions to the covenant people and to Jerusalem (Wildberger recognizes these as material 'welches sich von Haus aus auf... Israel bezog') are found in material and in phrases which are so closely identified solely with Jerusalem and the covenant people that to suggest that the author had redirected this material so that it currently applies to a universal context is, in effect, to misrepresent the significance of the allusions.[116] Nowhere else in the OT do we find Mosaic covenant terminology cast in a universal context. Nowhere else in the OT do we find an obvious epithet for Jerusalem (*mśwś h'rṣ*) reapplied to a worldwide setting. And very seldom in the rest of the OT do we find such terms of lament which occur in this passage applied to the distress of any nation other than Israel. When one adds to these observations (a) the evidence of an exegetical relationship between 24.8, 9 and 5.11-14, (b) the *double entendre* of the phrase, *bqrb h'rṣ*, and (c) the association of *mrwm* with Jerusalem, it becomes obvious that any universalistic reinterpretation which is imposed on this material only destroys its intended particularity. The signposts for Judah and Jerusalem may not be forced to point to the entire cosmos.

Having stated the case for the particularity of the author's focus, I also recognize that the author employs cosmic language, and even concludes his oracle of judgment with a depiction of the return to chaos (vv. 18-20). To be sure, this juxtaposition of the universal and the particular creates a certain tension that is not easily resolved. But the text resists resolution of the tension by the simple elimination of one of the two polarities.[117]

M.-L. Henry sought to resolve the seeming incongruity by suggesting that the author believed his own people (the particular) were *more* responsible for the worldwide judgment (the universal) than were the other peoples.[118] While this is a plausible view and has the merit of seeking to deal with the diversity of the material, it is unconvincing chiefly because there is nothing in the text which indicates a comparison of culpability.

2. *Chaos and Exile*

In my judgment, the tension within the text can best be understood in the light of the chaos myth to which the author alludes in v. 10 and vv. 18-20. It is important to observe how the entire portrayal of judgment is developed. The first unit (vv. 1-13) progresses with sharpening focus toward the city at the center of the earth which is reduced to *tōhû*. From this focal point, the author once again extends the imagery to include the entire cosmos (vv. 16b-20).[119] Clearly, the focus of these first twenty verses is on the city in v. 10. To a large degree the fate of the *ʾrṣ* is inextricably linked to the fate of the city. Once the city has been destroyed, then the encroachment of chaos is inevitable.

At the same time it must be observed that the description of the judgment is expansive. Initially, Yahweh's judgment is portrayed as a drought (vv. 4-7)[120] and/or famine that may be related to a siege (vv. 8, 9, 11). This is followed by the implication that an invading army will come (vv. 10, 12). Here, the term, *thw*, functions proleptically. The description of the city as *tōhû* is the adumbration of the encroachment of cosmic chaos that is depicted in vv. 18-20. It is only subsequent to the mention of the city's fate that the author expands the chaos imagery on a cosmic scale.

The pivotal role of the city in the description of the reversion of the cosmos to chaos makes sense if the city is Jerusalem. The people of God are taken into exile, the dwelling place of God is destroyed, and Yahweh himself must leave. This is chaos.

This prophet was not alone in viewing the historical events of devastation and exile in the mythic terms of chaos. Second Isaiah perceived the exile as a return to chaos, and the burden of his message was that this present moment of chaos was not Yahweh's intention for his people, nor would it continue for very long:

> For thus says the Lord, who created the heavens (he is God), who formed the earth and made it (he established it; he did not create it a chaos, he formed it to be inhabited): '... I did not say to the offspring of Jacob, "Seek me in chaos"' (Isa. 45.18, 19b).

In another passage Yahweh is reminded that he earlier had destroyed the chaos monster at the time of the exodus from Egypt in the creation of the people. Now in a similar time of chaos Yahweh is called upon to act on behalf of his people:

> Awake, awake, put on strength, O arm of the Lord;
> awake, as in the days of old,
> the generation of long ago.

Was it not thou that didst cut Rahab in pieces,
that didst pierce the dragon? (Isa. 51.9).

Finally, the poet connects the exile with the chaos myth by implication when he writes:

For a brief moment I forsook you, . . .
In overflowing wrath for a moment
I hid my face from you, . . .
For this is like the days of Noah to me (Isa. 54.7-9a).

And we may surmise that Second Isaiah's frequent references to Yahweh as creator (40.12ff.; 44.24; 45.13, 18; 51.13, 16) were, in part, attempts to assure the exiles that the one who created order out of chaos in primeval time is capable of doing it again in their own time.

Jeremiah is another prophet who connects the exile with a return to chaos. In reflecting on the invasion of Judah and destruction of Jerusalem by Nebuchanezzar, he portrays the effect of these events in Stygian terms which in themselves emote a sense of chaotic doom:

I looked on the earth, and lo,
it was waste and void (*tōhû wābōhû*);
and to the heavens and they had no light.
I looked on the mountains, and lo,
they were quaking (*r'šym*).
and all the hills moved to and fro.
I looked, and lo, there was no man,
and all the birds of the air had fled.
I looked, and lo, the fruitful land was a desert,
and all the cities were laid in ruins,
before Yahweh, before his fierce anger (Jer. 4.23-26).[121]

The near synonymity of exile and chaos is clear from these texts and has been recognized by most scholars.[122] And in my judgment the cosmic language of the chaos myth, to a large degree, explains the cosmic terminology that we find in Isa. 24.1-20 juxtaposed with the allusions to a particular people. But there is an additional aspect which A.J. Wensinck expresses as follows:

This thought is only to be understood, if we think of the Israelitic idea, that the history of the world is really only a history of Israel, as the nucleus of mankind[123]

In keeping with the Hebraic world view, this prophet wrote about the history of Israel *as if it were* the history of the world. If Israel's heart and center, Jerusalem, is reduced to chaos, then it is inevitable, to this way of thinking, that the whole cosmos will be reduced to chaos.

> This nucleus of mankind, according to the ancient conception, has its fixed place in the centre of the earth and this has been cleansed for it by its God, who Himself has His dwelling place amidst His people... And now the exile has destroyed this harmonious order of things: there is scarcely a people of Israel any more; it no longer dwells in the centre of the earth, on the place destined for it by its god; and this god himself has been driven away from his dwelling place, the temple of Jerusalem. This is really chaos.[124]

In my view, this understanding of the interrelationship of chaos and the exile as we have described it commends itself for the following two reasons: (a) it deals justly with both the universal and particular dimensions within the text without sacrificing one for the other (as is required with Wildberger's 'Uminterpretation'); (b) it is in keeping with the ideological milieu of sixth-century Judah, which is to say, on the one hand, that other sixth-century prophets gave expression to a similar correspondence between the exile and the chaos myth, while on the other hand, nowhere during this era do we find the notion, characteristic of later apocalyptic thought, that the entire age terminates in a universal destruction.[125] Therefore, I conclude that the author of 24.1-20 perceived with prophetic insight the impending destruction of his city and limned that destruction with its concomitant exile in the cosmic imagery of the chaos myth.

Chapter 3

THE VICTORY OF YAHWEH (ISAIAH 24.21–27.1)

A. *The Relationship between 24.21–27.1 and 24.1-20*[1]

Most interpreters agree that a new section begins with 24.21. The introductory formula, *whyh bywm hhw'*, and the change of mood from a sense of doom, destruction, and judgment (24.1-20) to one of jubilation, victory, and salvation support this view. But are these features such that they warrant the conclusion drawn by W.E. March that 24.1-20 and 24.21–27.1 are not two sections of one composition, but rather are two independent, and originally unrelated compositions?[2] In addition to the two points mentioned above (introductory formula and change of mood), he bases this position on the following features: (1) There are no points of contact between the two sections. (2)The principal motif of 24.21–27.1, which is the reign of Yahweh, is not found in 24.1-20. (3) The style is different.[3]

I must disagree with March for three reasons:

(a) He has failed to see that much of his evidence for diversity is actually an indication that the author has arranged the material in accordance with the pattern of the chaos myth which was well established across the ancient Near East. As one may readily observe from the Baal-Anat cycle or the Marduk-Tiamat myth, the pattern consistently is as follows: threat, victory, reign, feast.[4] For Isa. 24–27, the threat of chaos has been depicted in 24.1-20. The purpose of the ensuing verses is to portray the anticipated victory, reign, and feast of Yahweh. Thus, one expects, rather than is surprised by, the shift in mood which is evident in the two sections. Nor is one troubled by the introduction of the *new* motif of the reign of Yahweh: it conforms precisely to the pattern.

(b) Rather than there being no 'points of contact' between the two sections, as March has charged, we note two: (1) We demonstrated in the last chapter that the Hebrew phrases, *mśwś h'rṣ*, *bqrb h'rṣ*, and the term, *mrwm*, were veiled references to Jerusalem and Mt Zion (a point with which March agrees); the link with 24.23 and related passages is clear. (2) I see a connection between the communal lament in 26.7-19 and the description of judgment in 24.1-20: the situation of distress which is implied in 26.7-19 is identical with the one which is described in 24.1-20. The one presupposes the other.[5] If one posits two originally unrelated compositions (with March), then one is left with the lament in 26.7-19 which has no connection to the situation which gave rise to it, viz. 24.1-20. Indeed, it is my position that the entire oracle of deliverance (24.21–27.1) presupposes a situation from which the people of God need deliverance, namely, the destruction and exile which are described in 24.1-20.

(c) Finally, March suggests that the style in 24.21–27.1 is different from that in 24.1-20. But the use of repetition, chiasm, and *inclusio*[6] throughout 24.21–27.1 parallels that found in 24.1-20. Likewise, we note that the same use of alliteration, paronomasia, and assonance that we observed in 24.1-20 may be found in 24.21–27.1.[7] In short, the elements of style argue forcefully against March's position.

I conclude that 24.1-20 and 24.21–27.1 are not two compositions which originally were unrelated, but are two movements in a larger composition which is patterned after the well-known chaos conflict. The first section depicts the encroachment of chaos, while the second portion predicts the victory of Yahweh over the forces of chaos.

1. *The Function of* bywm hhw'

On the surface it is obvious that the introductory formula, *whyh bywm hhw'*, serves to connect the two sections of the composition. But the interpreter must be more precise. Is the expression intended to suggest that the events mentioned in 24.21ff. are to be seen as *parallel* to the day of judgment described in 24.1-20? Or does the phrase *bywm hhw'* indicate that the author has shifted his focus from the day of judgment to the distant future and a time of salvation?

In 1936 Peter Andreas Munch wrote a monograph entitled, *The Expression Bajjôm Hahû', Is it an Eschatological Terminus Technicus?*[8] His investigation was a specific challenge to H. Gressmann, who had concluded that the phrase always had an eschatological meaning.[9] The results of Munch's inquiry are summarized in one sentence: 'The expression wants everywhere to be understood as a temporal adverb'.[10] In his view it simply served as a connection between two pieces of literature. With specific reference to Isa. 24.21 he writes: 'It is meant to mark the transition between the two main sections of the apocalypsis. Of course, it must be conceived as a temporal adverb'.[11]

But Munch's work suffers because of the strictly literary approach which he employed. His work is an illustration of the claim which James Barr has made with striking, though mordant, clarity: a strictly linguistic approach to words or expressions may be very misleading.[12] Very few expressions in the OT allow themselves to be construed in the monochrome way in which Munch has portrayed the phrase *bywm hhw'*.

The work of Simon J. DeVries, which benefits from scholarly developments since 1936, marks a significant improvement on Munch's work.[13] In this treatise on time and history in the OT DeVries not only establishes a more comprehensive context for the phrase *bywm hhw'*, but he also takes note of the various types of literature in which it is located and the variety of functions the phrase is intended to perform.

DeVries' work connects most closely with our study in his treatment of the occurrences of *bywm hhw'* in the prophetic corpus (pp. 295-323). He organizes the uses into four categories: (a) glosses, (b) incorporating statements, (c) transitional formulae, (d) concluding formulae. Isa. 24.21ff. clearly belongs to category 'b'. Incorporating statements have the effect of *expanding* the original oracles to which the statements are attached.[14]

Taking DeVries' lead, I propose that *bywm hhw'* serves to extend the day of judgment on Judah by incorporating Yahweh's new action of salvation. Note the parallel texts:

1. Isa. 4.2. The oracle of judgment in Isa. 3.1–4.1 is expanded to include the announcement of salvation.
2. Isa. 27.12, 13. The lament over fallen Jerusalem in vv. 7-11 is followed by an announcement of the return of the exiles.
3. Isa. 28.5. The announcement of judgment against Ephraim is expanded to include a prophecy of Yahweh's benevolent reign.
4. Jer. 30.8. This pericope is very much like Isa. 24.21. Both are preceded by an announcement of unmitigated horror. Then, by means of the phrase, *bywm hhw'*, the day of judgment is expanded into a day of salvation, announcing Yahweh's destruction of the enemy and deliverance of Israel.

5. Amos 9.11. The prophet's pronouncement of destruction on his people is expanded to a prophecy of restoration.[15]

In each of these passages the day of judgment for Israel has been extended in order to indicate that judgment is not Yahweh's final word for Israel. Rather, Yahweh will act in the near future to effect the deliverance of Israel.

DeVries concludes his analysis by asking two pertinent questions: 'Is bayyôm hahû' a mechanical connective, joining two bodies of unrelated material, or does the redactor/editor have a particular purpose? . . . does it merely mean, "then", as Munch has so confidently affirmed?'[16] In my judgment his response is correct and to the point:

> Wherever bayyôm hahû is used to incorporate supplementary material, two actions, that of the original pericope and that of the secondary material, are equated in time, hence the synchronizing function. But we need to realize that the redactor was doing more. He was in effect *extending the day of the original pericope to include his new actions*, stretching it and coloring it to include new conditions. (Emphasis mine; later, he adds:) What then is 'that day' future? It is God's or man's new opportunity for decisive action. Although it may not be immediately present, like hayyôm or maḥar it is imminently certain.[17]

2. *Interpretation*

I stated in the previous chapter that 24.1-20 is the prediction of the destruction of Judah and Jerusalem written from the vantage point of the eve of that destruction, perhaps between the years 597-587. We may infer from the lament in 26.7-19 that some time has passed and the writer of 24.21–27.1 is in the midst of the exile. In his view, the word of judgment which Yahweh executed against his people will not be the final word. Therefore he extends the day of judgment in order to include an oracle of salvation. The correctness of this conclusion is supported by the stark contrast of mood between the two sections. In 24.1-20 we find mourning and languishing (vv. 4, 7), a somber sense of sin (vv. 5, 20), cessation of all joy (vv. 8, 11), and a cry of woe (v. 16b). But it is believed that all of this will be changed, and 24.21–27.1 presents the opposite picture: not mourning but exulting (25.1), not a sense of sin, but the removal of the 'reproach of his people' (25.8), not a cessation of joy, but a song of joy (26.1-16), not a cry of woe, but the wiping away of tears and the removal of death (25.8).

What motivated the prophet to transform 'the day' in this way? We can only speculate. We know that the OT writers shared the ancient Near Eastern *Weltanschauung* which held that chaos would be followed by order and a new era of salvation. Perhaps there was something taking place within the exilic situation which gave rise to a new hope for the future. Whatever the catalyst, the day of gloom was extended and transformed into a day of salvation.

It is difficult to determine with certainty if this later writer is the same one who authored the oracle of judgment (24.1-20). The similarity of style (the use of assonance, alliteration, paronomasia, repetition, inclusio, and chiasm)[18] between the two pieces certainly argues for one author of both, and there is no compelling reason to deny this view.

B. *The Triumph of Yahweh (24.21-23)*

1. *The Origin of the Pericope*

There is a general agreement that 24.21-23 comprises a unit. We have already noted those points which mark its beginning. The pericope reaches a climax with the mention of Yahweh reigning on Mt Zion, in Jerusalem. Finally, it is clear that the song in 25.1-5 marks a new unit.

Scholars are divided concerning the origin of this pericope. Plöger conveys the opinion of many when he describes 24.21-23 as 'an independent addition' added later when the reason behind 24.1-20 'was no longer so important or a different reason had made its appearance'.[19] In my judgment, Plöger's view demonstrates that he has misunderstood 24.1-20, for if, as we have suggested, hostile forces had destroyed Jerusalem, banished Yahweh from his city, and brought the earth to the brink of chaos, then it is entirely appropriate, within the ancient Near Eastern worldview, to portray Yahweh as striking out against the hostile forces and returning to reign in the city of his choosing.

Plöger is not alone in his assessment of these verses. Wildberger holds that they are a later interpolation because of the formula *whyh bywm hhw'*, which is generally recognized as introducing later material (but see our discussion above, pp. 49f.).[20] Lindblom and Kaiser concur with Wildberger's view.[21]

While I am not convinced by Plöger and others that vv. 21-23 are a later interpolation, I am troubled by: (1) the sudden change from *'rṣ*, which occurred sixteen times in the first twenty verses without exception, to *'dmh*; (2) the abrupt change of emphasis from the earth to the other worldly bodies.

The second point may be attributed to the influence of the pattern of the *Chaoskampf*, but the first point suggests that the author was borrowing from a different source. Perhaps Plöger is on the right track when he refers to these verses as, '"eschatologoumena" from a traditional repertoire, which there were reasons for not wishing to bypass'.[22] But I must disagree with the assessment that these verses are 'later', because that would require an original juxtaposition of 24.1-20 with 25.1-5 or 25.6-8, which would have been impossible in either instance. Rather, this pericope, perhaps derived from an older body of material and modified by the author, was then employed to introduce the announcement of the victory of Yahweh and the deliverance of his people.

2. *The Defeat of the Hostile Powers*

The expression *ṣb' hmrwm* has elicited numerous conjectures as to its identity. Ibn Ezra, Duhm, Gray, Procksch, Rudolph, and Kaiser interpret the phrase in the light of Dan. 10.13, 21 as a reference to the angels which protect a nation.[23] J. Lindblom, reading the phrase in the light of the book of *Enoch*, regarded this as a reference to angelology: 'Unsere Stelle hängt offenbar mit spätjüdischen angelologischen und eschatologischen Vorstellungen zusammen'.[24] F. Delitzsch thought this could refer either to 'the starry host (40.26) or the angelic host (1 Kgs 22.19; Ps. 148.2)', but because of the parallel term *mlky*, which 'designates personal powers', he inferred that the author intended the angelic host.[25] J. Calvin viewed the phrase as a reference to earthly powers.[26] Finally, Wildberger, Kessler, Henry, Fohrer, and Kissane regard the expression as a reference either to stars or astral worship (Deut. 4.19; 17.3; 2 Kgs 17.16; 23.11ff.; Jer. 19.13; Ps. 33.6; Isa. 40.26) or to gods (1 Kgs 22.19; Job 1.6).[27]

It is obvious from the above survey that, in general, those who date this material late interpret it in the light of the book of Daniel and/or the book of *Enoch*, while those who date it early see another tradition as influential. As we noted in the introduction, there is an emerging consensus that the date of the composition belongs closer to the exile than it does to the time of the writing of the book of Daniel.[28] Therefore it is unlikely that the expression, *ṣb' hmrwm*, reflects a nascent angelology.

I suggest that in the light of the already established relationship between Isa. 24–27 and the mythical language of the *Chaoskampf*, we look to this mythological motif for traditional antecedents. A portion of *Enuma eliš* is strikingly parallel to 24.21-23. After Marduk had defeated Tiamat, he pursued her attendant gods and made them captive:

> After he had slain Tiamat, the leader, Her band was shattered, her troupe broken up; And the gods, her helpers who marched at her side, Trembling with terror, turned their backs about. In order to save and preserve their lives. Tightly encircled, they could not escape. He made them captives and he smashed their weapons. Thrown into the net, they found themselves ensnared; Placed in cells, they were filled with wailing; Bearing his wrath, they were held imprisoned (Table IV, lines 105-114).[29]

This suggests that the *ṣb' hmrwm* of 24.21 are other gods. But may we define thes 'gods' more precisely? Note the parallel expression, *mlky h'dmh*. There is a distinct connection between the gods and the nations, a connection which is also evidenced in Psalm 82, Jer. 46.25 and Zeph. 2.11. The last reference is particularly pertinent:

> Yahweh will be terrible against them;
> yea, he will famish all the gods of the earth,
> and to him shall bow down, each in its place,
> all the lands of the nations.

This suggests that in 24.21-23, the author has employed language which is typically associated with the enthronement of Yahweh.[30] Because this is typical language, it is inappropriate to try to establish the precise identity of the enemy forces on the basis of this pericope.

Verse 23 suggests that the gods were perceived as heavenly bodies. Most interpreters view this verse as having no connection with the destruction of the gods in v. 21; rather, they maintain, the clause serves only as a foil to highlight the brightness of the *kbwd* of Yahweh.[31] But Wildberger has correctly observed that the terms *hpr* and *bwš* are not what one would expect to be used for this purpose, since they do not mean 'to become pale', or the equivalent. Both words are much stronger, focusing on the *shame* experienced by the two heavenly bodies. Thus, the polemical function is not to be denied.[32]

The point of the pericope is that Yahweh, on the day of his

appearing, will destroy any power which is against him, and having defeated that power, he will resume his reign on Mt Zion. As with Jer. 46.25 and Zeph. 2.11, typical, theophanic language is employed.

3. *The Purpose of the Phrase 'And after many days'*
This phrase has been a source of difficulty for interpreters. Calvin spiritualized it, suggesting that, 'It was intended to try the faith of the godly; for we are hasty in our desires, and would wish that God should immediately perform his promises'.[33] Lindblom queried, 'Wie kann nach dem Endgericht, von dem hier offenbar die Rede ist, noch ein Gericht "nach vielen Tagen" den schon Gerichteten bevorstehen?' He concluded that v. 22 contains two separate strands regarding the judgment of the evil powers that have been conjoined.[34] But surely he is treating the poetry too rigidly.

In my view there are two possibilities for the function of this phrase: (1) It may be a literary technique designed to heighten the suspense involved in Yahweh's overthrow of the powers. (2) It may be an attempt to caution the readers that the period of waiting is not yet over. Even though the announcement of Yahweh's victory is now being made, the reality of deliverance has not yet been effected. *De jure* has not yet become *de facto*. Thus, there is an emphasis on *trust* in the subsequent material (25.9; 26.3, 4). The author, while assuring his readers of Yahweh's triumph, by means of the phrase *wmrb ymym*, cautions them that it may not come as soon as they might wish.[35]

The Reign of Yahweh on Mt Zion
It is not my intention here to enter the discussion between S. Mowinckel, G. von Rad, H.J. Kraus, and others on the original setting of the Day of Yahweh.[36] What is clear is that when Yahweh has vanquished his foes, the forces of chaos, he will return to his city and reign supreme on his holy mountain. The implication is that Yahweh had *not* been reigning in Jerusalem.[37] No doubt the events of 587 had brought into serious question the viability of Yahweh's kingship.

What calls for attention precisely because it is unanticipated is the phrase, 'before his elders'. While this is an obvious allusion to Exod. 24.9-11, its function is not so obvious. It may have had a polemical function, showing a distinct preference for one group within the community as leaders of the people. This would be in keeping with

Hanson's suggestion that, 'the alienated and oppressed classes look to the more distant past for models which call into question the position of power claimed by the ruling classes'.[38] But this view assumes an internal tension which cannot be supported from the text.

I propose that the mention of the elders serves to recall the covenant ratification between Yahweh and Israel. The new appearance of Yahweh before his elders dramatizes the fact that he has extended to his people, once again, the covenant which had been broken (24.5).[39]

C. *A Song of Thanksgiving (25.1-5)*

1. *The Song's Integrity and Function in the Composition*

Nearly all interpreters agree that vv. 1-5 form a literary unit, and that the pericope is a song of thanksgiving, or *Danklied*.[40] Only Lohmann disagrees, calling it a 'religiöses Siegeslied'.[41] More significant for the history of interpretation of this pericope and the composition as a whole has been the *communis opinio* that 25.1-5 (along with 26.1-6) was originally 'independent and distinct' from the rest of Isa. 24–27, and referred to the destruction of a fallen city in the past. Lohmann expresses the implications of this view in this fashion:

> Darüber, daß 25.1-5 eine literarische Einheit bilden, herrscht nur eine Meinung. Sind doch von diesem Stücke—*eben seiner Selbständigkeit wegen*—die Zweifel an der Einheitlichkeit von Jes. 24–27 ausgegangen.[42]

Wildberger is of the same mind: 'Darin bestätigt sich, daß es nicht zur Grundschicht gehört und erst recht nicht von Haus aus zwischen 24.21-23 und 25.6-8 gestanden haben kann'.[43] But due to his keen theological sense he maintains that in the process of theological interpretation one must view the song in terms of its function in its present location, i.e. in the context of two, future-oriented pericopae.[44]

O. Plöger disagrees with this latter point. Noting that the song is 'independent and distinct from the surrounding verses', he insists that it is to be 'interpreted separately and independently' as well.[45] This has been the majority view since B. Duhm stated that the key to understanding the 'Isaiah Apocalypse' was the separation of the material into two categories: (1) eschatological prophecies and (2) songs which describe a past event.[46] The above views more often than not have been only stated rather than adequately defended. Rudolph was the first to challenge the prevailing position. He maintained that 25.1-5 did not have a prior existence but was composed for its present context. His reasoning is twofold: (1) 25.6-8 did *not* follow directly on 24.21-23:

> Wie können plötzlich 'alle Völker' zum eschatologischen Freudenmahl kommen . . .? Der notwendige Zwischengedanke, daß das Vorgehen Jahwes auf die Völker Eindruck macht und ihr Verhältnis zu ihm verändert, steht in 25.3. Somit war 25.1-5 von vornherein für die Stelle bestimmt, die es jetzt einnimmt.[47]

(2) He states that 25.1-5 presupposes that Yahweh is reigning on Mt Zion (24.23) as indicated by the phrase in v. 4, *mḥsh mzrm ṣl mḥrb*. Rudolph reckoned this to be a reference to Isa. 4.6, which states that Yahweh, *reigning on Mt Zion*, creates a shade from the heat and a shelter from the storm.[48]

Rudolph's view is complemented by the work of O. Kaiser, who insists that v. 3 casts the entire pericope in a futuristic mood by referring to the 'conversion of the nations to Yahweh at the end time' (cf. Ps. 86.9).[49] Therefore, he maintains, it is fruitless and contrary to the intention of the author to look for an event in the past. Secondly, a consideration of the formal characteristics of the song has led Kaiser to conclude:

> this passage is not a psalm of thanksgiving taken from a different context, but a prophetic song of thanksgiving composed specifically for its present place. The poet, thoroughly familiar with the language of the psalms, expresses in this way his firm conviction that the unknown city, which like Babylon in chs. 13 and 14 is a symbol of the whole concentration of power hostile to God, will one day be annihilated, and anticipates the thanksgiving for this. But because the event still lies in the future and very little of Yahweh's power can be observed at the present moment, he begins with a confident profession of faith in Yahweh.[50]

In my view, the arguments of Rudolph and Kaiser are convincing. The song in 25.1-5 is not a later intrusion but was composed for its present location. This conclusion has several implications:

1. It brings to an end the schema introduced by Duhm which would fragment the composition into independent and unrelated segments. A more comprehensive approach is required.

2. It means that it is no longer necessary that the identity of the city accord precisely with the description given in 25.1-5. This is a prediction of a future action rather than a description of a past event.
3. It suggests that, for the author, there is a connection between a future historical event and the introduction of the new, eschatological age. The realm of history has not yet been abandoned for the cosmic dualism of the later apocalypticists.[51]

2. The Identity of the Hostile City

From 25.1-5 we learn three things about the enemy city.

(1) It is bitterly hated by the prophet. From v. 2 we note that the writer is not content simply to announce the city's demise, rather he adds phrase after phrase which, in crescendo-like fashion, points to the finality of the fate of this city, and reflects the emotional intensity of the author rather than the accuracy of his prediction. If we are correct in understanding 24.1-20 as a description of the fall of Jerusalem, then we may assume that the immediate mention of a hostile city, indeed the prediction of the everlasting devastation of that enemy city within the context of an oracle of salvation for Israel, suggests that the despised city was the same one which was responsible for the destruction of Jerusalem.

(2) The mention of the enemy city in immediate connection with Yahweh's defeat of the hostile powers (24.21-23), and the introduction of the eschatological age (25.6-10a) suggest that this city was perceived as embodying all the anti-godly powers which must be destroyed before the new age could dawn.

(3) The city's influence was worldwide. Its destruction would affect all the nations (cf. 25.3).

From Jewish perspective there was only one city which would fit this description: Babylon. To be sure, during their history the Jews despised several enemy cities, but they did not believe that the overthrow of any of these other cities would have the impact portrayed here. Certainly they did not believe this of Samaria,[52] Carthage,[53] or any Moabite city.[54] But they did believe this about Babylon. Second Isaiah repeatedly asserts that Babylon's end will mark a new beginning; the beginning of the new age when the nations will turn to Yahweh (Isa. 40.6; 42.10-13; 45.20-23; 48.14; 49.1, 6, 7, 25, 26; 55.5). Babylon was known to have a worldwide influence (13.19; 14.6, 7; 47.5; Jer. 50.23, 46; 51.7, 41, 48). Further, the intensity with which the Jews abhorred Babylon is well known. As J. Bright notes:

> no power in ancient times affected the fortunes of Israel in a more catastrophic way than did Babylon. It is, therefore, not to be wondered at that many a Jew came to look upon Babylon as the very arch-foe of the people of God.[55]

It is not surprising then that several scholars have proposed Babylon as the city in question: M.-L. Henry, the capture of Babylon by Cyrus in 538;[56] J. Lindblom, the 'destruction' of Babylon by Xerxes in 485;[57] and W. Rudolph, the capture of Babylon by Alexander the Great in 331.[58]

Lindblom has mounted the most sustained argument for identifying the hostile city as Babylon. For the most part his analysis is correct, though two major errors led to his erroneous dating: (1) He assumed that the city was the same throughout the composition (in 24.10; 25.2; 26.5, 6; 27.10).[59] Therefore, he mistakenly gleaned data from 24.10 and 27.10 and applied it to Babylon. (2) He failed to realize that both 25.1-5 and 26.1-6 were composed for their present locations and must be viewed as referring to a *future* event. Therefore, he mistakenly connected both pericopae with a past event.

Once it is recognized that the defeat of the enemy power lies in the future then it is no longer necessary that the specific details accord with the historical events. This is particularly important because of the objection that the author could not have been referring to the overthrow of Babylon by Cyrus in 538 since the city was not destroyed at that time. Indeed we might reasonably argue as Bright did regarding the dating of Jeremiah 50 and 51, that because the 'description' of the destruction does not square with the actuality it is 'unthinkable' that it had been composed after the event.[60]

There is one other factor that argues against the later dating of Lindblom (and Rudolph). By 485 (and certainly by 331) Babylon was no longer a world power. It no longer controlled the destiny of the Jews. Nor would its demise at this later time be considered to have the universal effects which are depicted in this composition. Further, the later literature of Israel (5th and 4th centuries) does not seem to focus on or allude to Babylon in any way similar to what we have in 25.2 or Isaiah 13, 14, 47 and Jeremiah 50 and 51. To be sure, the name 'Babylon' took on a symbolic dimension in later periods of oppression such as those found in the books of Daniel and

Revelation. But the symbolic dimension arose in part because the historical city with its awesome power had gone into eclipse.

We noted above (p. 29) that a comparison of 24.7-12 and 25.1-5 highlighted the differences between the two pericopae. In the former the destruction is described in terms of a lament and the mood is sombre, while in the latter, the language is that of a song and the mood is one of jubilation. The differences may be traced still further. In each passage the ruination of the city triggers a chain of events. In 24.7-12 the city's reduction to *tōhû* (chaos) adumbrates the reversal of the cosmos to chaos. Incalculable devastation ensued from the city's demise. But the picture is completely different with the destruction of the city in 25.1-5. It will lead to immeasurable beneficence. The nations will turn to Yahweh. The poor and needy will be cared for.[61] Yahweh will reign on Mt Zion. Chaos will return to cosmos. And the golden age will have arrived. There can be little doubt that we are dealing with two different cities. And for the Jewish mind, the destruction of Jerusalem alone could lead to a collapse into chaos, while only the destruction of Babylon could initiate the new eschatological age.

D. *Yahweh's Victory Feast (25.6-10a)*

1. *Delimiting the Unit*

There is no consensus as to the length of the next pericope. It is variously considered to be vv. 6-8, 6-10a, and 6-12. Those who divide after v. 8 do so on the basis off the concluding formula, ***ky yhwh dbr***, in v. 8 and the introductory formula, ***w'mr bywm hhw'***, in v. 9.[62] More specifically, DeVries thinks the ineptness of the introductory formula in v. 9 is evidence for the unit being a later editorial addition.[63] But Procksch argues that a consistent meter throughout vv. 6-10a is a basis for its unity.[64] Lindblom also divides after v. 10a and substantiates this by appealing to the *inclusio* formed by ***bhr hzh*** in vv. 6 and 10a.[65]

The evidence is significant for both positions. But in my judgment the *inclusio* (***bhr hzh***) implies that the author[66] regarded the entirety of vv. 6-10a as a unit. This is not to deny the formal characteristics which mark off vv. 9-10a, but to indicate that it may be more appropriate to designate them as a separate strophe within the larger unit.

2. *The Universal and the Particular*

In the light of the Ugaritic material which has played a significant role in the background of Isa. 24–27, it is of particular interest to note for whom Yahweh makes the feast. While Baal made a feast for the other gods, Yahweh extends the invitation to all peoples. Further, in contrast to those passages which portray *h'mym* as humbled subjects,[67] this pericope elevates them to an unprecedented status. Thus, Wildberger is correct in noting that the author not only has eschatologized the coronation meal, but also has broadened it to include all people.[68]

The universalism could scarcely be more evident, though there are those who construe this passage to yield a strict nationalism. One of the first (mis)interpretations of this sort is found in the Targum:

> And the Lord of hosts shall make for all nations in this mountain a feast and a festival; they shall consider that it is given for their honor but it shall be for their shame, even plagues from which they cannot escape, plagues wherein they will perish.[69]

More recently, Redditt has maintained that there is no hint of universalism in these verses. His reasoning is twofold: (1) Israel is elevated. (2) The inclusion of the Moab pericope was intended as a symbolic reference to 'those enemies of Israel who are to be banned from Jerusalem'.[70]

Redditt's argument regarding the Moab pericope is unconvincing. We have already demonstrated that the pericope is a later interpolation. Further, we note that the destruction of the enemy of Israel was the focus of 25.1-5, an event which would lead to the conversion of the nations and their inclusion at the great feast. A mood of compassion for all peoples pervades the passage in 25.6-10. And it is this context of conciliation which requires the exclusion of the Moab pericope rather than the exclusion Moab from among the nations gathered at the victory feast.

Secondly, Redditt cites the 'elevation of Israel' as evidence of a strong nationalism. But one must be careful to distinguish between particularity and nationalism. It is possible to maintain the uniqueness and identity of Israel on the one hand while holding to the universal inclusion of all nations under the canopy of God's grace on the other. This 'fruitful paradox'[71] is given expression in Isa. 2.2f. and 55.5, and is essential for Paul's presentation of a universal gospel which at the same time insists on the particularity and priority of Israel.[72]

It will be noted further that the author has arranged the themes of universality and particularity in a contrapuntal relationship. The catholicity of 'all peoples', 'all nations', 'all faces', and 'all the earth', is interchanged with the particular notions of 'this mountain', 'his people', and 'our God'. The effect is such that it suggests that Yahweh's actions on behalf of his particular people will result in universal salvation.[73]

Rudolph, Lindblom, and Plöger have noted the oddity of a reference to 'all peoples', in the light of 24.1-20 which, according to their view, states that only a very few people will survive the coming devastation of the world.[74] Rudolph and Lindblom try to circumvent this difficulty by reasoning that the lack of harmonization of details is to be attributed to the nature of the eschatological material.[75] The problem is less acute for Plöger, who thinks of these as 'independent units' for which 'occasional inconsistencies are not felt to be disruptive'.[76]

But the dissonance which is fostered by such an interpretation may not be treated so cursorily. One simply cannot do away with the inconsistencies by appealing to the 'nature of the material'. Indeed, the mention of the near total destruction of humanity on the one hand (24.1-20) and the invitation of 'all peoples' on the other (25.6; cf. also the conversion of the nations in 25.3) creates such an internal tension that it is doubtful that any author would be comfortable with it. However, if 24.1-20 is interpreted as I have proposed, namely, as the destruction of Jerusalem, then there is no conflict with the mention of 'all peoples' in 25.8.

We owe to M.-L. Henry the elaboration of a motif that goes back at least as far as Wilhelm Vatke, namely, that there is an inherent connection betwen the exile and the development of the understanding of Yahweh as a universal God.[77] Henry notes that the exile, which meant the loss of both the homeland and the national existence must have aroused the thought among the Jews that Yahweh either had forsaken them or he would overthrow the gods of the conquering power and become the god of the entire world.[78] Elsewhere, in commenting on the relationship between 24.21-23 and 25.6-8, she writes:

> daß dem Leitbild des Königs noch nach dem *nationalen Zusammenbruch* ein so starkes Faszinosum innewohnte, daß die ganze Fülle einer universalen Gottesvorstellung in sich aufzunehmen vermöchte . . . (emphasis mine)[79]

Even though Henry interprets 24.1ff. as a worldwide destruction, by mentioning the 'national disaster' in this context, she unwittingly supports my interpretation of that material.

Delitzsch and Procksch are among the few scholars who maintain that the covering and veil are symbolic expressions for spiritual blindness.[80] But the prior mention of the conversion of the nations indicates that the spiritual blindness had already been removed. Most interpreters are correct in seeing v. 7 as evidence that in the new age Yahweh will remove the sorrow and grief (2 Sam. 15.30; Jer. 14.3f.; Esth. 6.12) which have been a part of the human experience from the beginning.[81] The bliss of the new age is epitomized by the removal of death.

3. *The Removal of Death*

Until recently it has been commonplace to regard the first three words of v. 8 as a later interpolation.[82] But in my judgment the reasons for such a view are less than convincing. Lindblom mentions three reasons: (1) Rhythmically, the phrase goes with neither the preceding nor the following material. (2) The lack of a conjunction, *waw*, is striking. (3) The repetition of the verb *bl'* is disruptive 'geschmacklos'.[83] Taking these objections in reverse order, we note (1) with Millar that *bl'* is used very effectively to form an *inclusio* with *bl'* in v. 7, and gives the pericope shape.[84] (2) The conjunction, *waw*, was probably part of the original text. (3) As Millar has demonstrated, the rhythm is simply not a problem.[85]

Kaiser reasons that the phrase is a gloss because it 'interrupts the direct continuity of thought between v. 7 and v. 8a'.[86] But one should see v. 8a as the 'hinge' on which both v. 7 and v. 8 turn. The swallowing of death is the essential factor which ultimately makes possible the removal of sorrow, pain, and tears. Kaiser undermines his own argument, for later he writes that 'the later redactor has correctly interpreted the preceding verses when he adds that God will abolish death itself'.[87] Is it not more reasonable to assume that the original author 'correctly interpreted' his own material?

Finally, Plöger excises the phrase, because 'the passage is dealing with the destiny and future of nations and peoples rather than the fate and death of the individual'.[88] But his view assumes an impossibly sharp distinction between individuals and nations, and that *hmwt* refers strictly to individual resurrection, which is incorrect.

Biblical critics, for the most part, have assumed that 25.8a was a reference to the resurrection of the individual. Because they had made prior assumptions which led them to consider the 'Isaiah Apocalypse' as contemporaneous with the book of Daniel, they tended to interpret 25.8a in light of Dan. 12.2, which clearly is a reference to individual resurrection. But since it is now recognized that Isa. 24–27 is significantly earlier than the book of Daniel, the interpreter must look elsewhere for an interpretive key.

We have already noted the striking parallels between the Ugaritic Baal-Anat cycle and Isa. 24–27. According to the Canaanite myth, even though Baal had defeated Prince Yam, the chaos monster, his victory was not yet complete. There remained one more power with which he must contend: Mot, the ruler of the underworld. But in this battle, Baal is no match for Mot, who defeats him almost without struggle:

> (One lip to ea)rth, one lip to heaven,
> (He stretched out his) tongue to the stars.
> Baal entered his mouth,
> Descended into his maw.[89]

This imaginative depiction of Mot swalling Baal very likely provides the backdrop for the statement in 25.8a.

Given this background, the phrase *wbl' hmwt lnṣḥ* acquires special significance. (1) It acts as a polemic against the Canaanite religion. (2) It becomes an expression of trust: while Baal's victory over the hostile powers was incomplete and temporary, Yahweh's victory will be absolute and forever. (3) In the Ugaritic literature Mot was a divine power which threatened the life of the ruling deity and his purposes for creation. When Mot reigned, the land lay dormant under his dominion. While in Isa. 25.8 Mot is no longer deified, it does represent a power which is hostile to Yaweh's plan for his creation. The enthroned Yahweh cannot fully reign until every hostile power is destroyed.[90] He cannot inaugurate the new, golden age until he removes every threat to the new reality of *Heil*. And the context for 25.8a suggests that only when this last enemy is destroyed will the salvation which Yahweh intends for his people be complete.

In sum, the phrase *wbl' hmwt lnṣḥ* does not refer to individual resurrection, but to the defeat of the hostile powers. In my judgment, the readers of this pericope would have seen it solely as a statement of confidence assuring them that Yahweh would indeed reign, and the new, eschatological age surely would come. This is, in fact, what v. 9 states. Neither the readers nor the author would have imagined the notion of individual resurrection.[91]

4. *The Removal of Judah's Reproach*

Generally, the term for reproach, *ḥrp*, is associated with the exile, and this is always so when reference is made to the *scope* of the reproach (e.g. 'among the nations', 'to all the kingdoms of the earth'), as it is presented in 25.8: 'from all the earth'.[92] The removal of the reproach meant the termination of the exile.

Wildberger suggests that *wḥrph 'mw* refers to Judah's sense of being a minority among the peoples; it is similar to the 'antisemitism' reflected in the book of Esther, though he acknowledges that the normal meaning of *ḥrp* is connected with the loss of the homeland and national existence.[93] And one would surely hope for more supportive evidence than simply the book of Esther.

Similarly, Kaiser thinks that *ḥrp* refers to the ongoing foreign domination long after the exile. But the references which he adduces are unanimous in referring to the exile.[94] Gray makes no comment on the term at all.[95]

According to our interpretation of the composition, it makes excellent sense to regard *ḥrp* as an allusion to the exile. 24.1-20 depicts both the destruction of Judah and Jerusalem and the ensuing exile. This is followed by an announcement of deliverance: Yahweh will defeat the forces of chaos and will reign on Mt Zion, inaugurating the new age (24.23–25.8a). From the prophet's point of view, Yahweh's victory and return to Mt Zion meant the end of the exile and thus, the removal of Judah's reproach. Undoubtedly, future generations within Judaism would see this as a promise to them, that one day in the final triumph of Yahweh their misfortunes would be reversed, but the original provenance was the situation of exile.

5. *An Exhortation to Trust*

Verse 9 is an indirect exhortation to the oppressed community to assume a posture of trust and expectation, an indirect word of assurance that Yahweh would act as he had promised. Plöger correctly perceives this emphasis, but because he lifts the verse out of its context (he thinks v. 9 is 'independent' and 'not to be linked too closely with 25.6-8') he misinterprets its function as, 'the response of those who have hope, who are willing to go to meet the coming catastrophe in reliance upon Yahweh'.[96] But where is there any mention of a 'coming catastrophe' in the immediate context? The possibilities for this type of free-wheeling interpretation are limitless. Surely the interpreter must be guided by the present text and assume that the author had sufficient reason for locating the text in this particular context. Following an announcement of salvation, an exhortation to trust Yahweh to effect the promised deliverance seems entirely appropriate (cf. Isa. 40.31). The exhortation is strengthened by the concluding phrase introduced by the deictic particle, *kî*: *ky tnwḥ yd yhwh bhr hzh* (v. 10a).

yd yhwh is an expression used frequently in the Isaianic tradition to symbolize Yahweh's power,[97] and in this case, his ability to accomplish the deliverance which has been promised. E.J. Young has argued that v. 10 marks a change from Mt Zion to the mountainous terrain of Moab. In his view, the expression *tnwh yd yhwh* conveys a note of judgment: 'upon the mountain land of Moab His hand rests heavily and will press down Moab underneath Him'.[98] But surely Young is incorrect. Normally *nḥh* indicates a beneficent relationship (11.2), while a verb other than *nḥh* is employed to express judgment (as in 26.11, *yhwh rmh ydk*).[99]

E. *A Song of Trust (26.1-6)*

1. *Determination of the Unit and the Gattung*

There is no unanimity as to the *terminus ad quem* of the first unit in ch. 26. On one end of the spectrum are Duhm and Gray who extend the unit through v. 19.[100] At the other end is P. Lohmann who marks three divisions in the first six verses: vv. 1b-3 (*Mauerweihfestlied*),[101] vv. 4-5a (religious victory song),[102] vv. 5b-6 (redactional addition).[103] In between, Lindblom divides after v. 14,[104] while the majority of scholars make a division at v. 6.[105]

To a large degree I share the sentiments of Gray and Duhm that the poem, in its present form, demonstrates integrity throughout the first nineteen verses. It is, in the words of Duhm, 'vollgepfropft mit Assonanzen, Wortspielen u. dgl'.[106] And Gray is correct in recognizing that most alleged points of discontinuity are 'studied transitions'.[107] In the final analysis there is an overall sense of homogeneity. But in my view, the transition at v. 6 is significant enough to make a formal distinction between the song of trust (vv. 1-6) and the lament which follows. There are four reasons for arriving at this conclusion: (1)

verse 7 begins a direct address to Yahweh; (2) concatenation begins in a consistent pattern with v. 7 (7, 8, 9, 10) and not earlier; (3) the motif of contrast between the strong city and trampled city concludes with v. 6; (4) the perspective in vv. 1-6 is future while that of vv. 7-19 is present.[108]

The *Gattung* of 26.1-6 has been variously designated as a hymn of praise,[109] a *Danklied*,[110] a religious victory song coupled with an entrance song,[111] or a hymn.[112] In my judgment, none of these captions adequately reflects the prominent note of trust that characterizes this song. A careful study of the song reveals that vv. 3 and 4, which constitute a call to trust, are pivotal between the contrastive beginning and ending; the opening verses anticipate the construction of the strong city (vv. 1, 2), while the closing verses look to the destruction of the wicked city (vv. 5, 6).[113]

That the perspective of the song is futuristic is indicated by the superscription, *bywm hhw' ywšr hšyr hzh b'rṣ yhwdh*. Formally, the call to trust (vv. 3, 4) represents a replacement of the normal call to praise and thanksgiving. This suggests again that the song has been created for this particular context and does not refer to the destruction of a city in the past.[114] H. Wildberger essentially acknowledges this point when he writes that the 'theologische Mitte' is not found in the praise of God, but in the call to trust Yahweh forever.[115] But a call to trust is, by its very nature, future-oriented. It is inconsistent for Wildberger to write that on one level the song reflects a past experience, but on another level it looks to the future.

In summary, the song of trust looks ahead to two future events: the construction of the walls of Jerusalem and the destruction of the hostile city. That these events lie in the future may be defended on formal grounds, namely the construction of the song as a song of trust. This view may also be defended on historical grounds. Given the distress of those who witnessed the efforts to rebuild the city of Jerusalem and the temple ('Is it not in your sight as nothing?' Hag. 2.3), it is doubtful that the exuberance reflected in 26.1, 2 could have been shown after the fact.[116]

2. *The Purpose of the Song of Trust*

Why was a song of trust thought to be necessary at this point? The author had announced the victory of Yahweh over the hostile powers (24.21-23), concretizing this by predicting the destruction of a particular wicked city (25.1-5). This would mark the introduction of Yahweh's universal reign which would know no end because the final enemy would be destroyed (25.6-8). But at the time of writing the community was still poor (*dl*) and needy (*'bywn*) and in distress (*bṣr*). They continued to lament their present condition (26.7-19 is a communal lament). The chasm between the golden age of the future and the agonizing reality of the present required a bridge of trust, which would keep alive the hopes of the oppressed community.[117]

Millar has argued that the occasion of the song in 26.1-6 was the enthronement of Yahweh marked by 'the processional entrance of the Ark'.[118] Such a procession, he maintains, would serve to celebrate the victory of Yahweh the Divine Warrior over the forces of chaos. Without engaging in the debate between Mowinckel and H.J. Kraus as to whether or not such an enthronement festival actually occurred in Israel,[119] I would argue that any mooring which v. 2 might have had with an original enthronement setting has now been severed as the verse becomes part of the expression of trust. And any original reference to Yahweh's entering the gates (cf. Pss. 24.7-9; 132.8)[120] has been deleted in order to emphasize the 'righteous nation which keeps faith'. The focus on Yahweh's kingship had been brought to a close with 25.8. And with 25.9 the emphasis had already shifted to the community and their need to trust.[121]

Kaiser is entirely correct when he summarizes the main point of this song:

> If only you go on trusting firmly and unshakeably in Yahweh, then it will actually come about that you will enter Jerusalem as his liberated people, because he has destroyed the world power and world capital, and you who are now defenceless will be able to destroy every trace of it.[122]

The destruction of a world capital which leads to the liberation of the Jews and allows them to return to Jerusalem fits only one era in the history of Judah prior to the second century: the exile. Subsequent to the overthrow of Babylon by Cyrus, there is nothing in the literature of the OT which would link the overthrow of a world capital to the return of the Jewish people to Jerusalem.

There are some who insist that 26.6, which mentions the destruction of the world city at the hands (or feet) of the people of Judah, makes it impossible to consider Babylon as the hostile city since at no time did the Jewish community participate in the overthrow of Babylon. But it must be recognized that the song (as was the song in 25.1-5) was written prior to the events of 539, and in its setting was intended to convey a theme: the mighty would be brought down and the weak would be elevated. According to the Isaianic tradition this was characteristic of the epiphany of Yahweh (Isa. 2.12-22). Concern for historical accuracy was peripheral.

F. *The Lament of the Community (26.7-19)*

1. *The Extent and Integrity of the Unit*

Most scholars agree that this unit is an integrated whole and exhibits the characteristics of a lament. Eissfeldt has stated the general opinion: it is 'a prayer rather like a national lament'.[123]

There are two scholars who take exception to the prevailing view: Rudolph (followed by Kessler),[124] and Lindblom.[125] Rudolph, excercising an a priori assumption that vv. 14a and 19 refer to individual resurrection and are therefore late, forces a substantial rearrangement of the text: 26.12, 15-18, 13, 14b, 20, 21. All of the resurrection passages are placed together as a later addition: 26.14a, 18b, 19.[126] Of course there is no textual support for this creative orchestration of the text and very few have followed him. The task of the biblical interpreter is not to create a text which accords with his prior notions, but to try to understand the received text.

Lindblom makes a major division after v. 14. He argues that vv. 1-14 comprise a *Danklied*, and insists that he is following the guidelines which Gunkel had isolated for this form.[127] Interestingly, however, Gunkel described the section, 26.8-19a (excluding vv. 14b, 15) as a 'Klagelied des Volkes'.[128] Lindblom is able to arrive at his conclusion only by a forced analysis. He finds the *Dankformel* in v. 13! A warning to others to trust Yahweh is to be found in v. 4 (though this is a communication *within* the community!). The reason for the thanksgiving is stated in vv. 5, 6 and repeated at the end, vv. 11-14. Verses 7-10 provide a description of the ways of Yahweh. Finally, v. 15 begins something entirely new: a lament, so that in Lindblom's view vv. 1-14 and vv. 15ff. are independent units.[129]

It is not surprising that no one has seconded Lindblom's proposal. In addition to the forced reasoning of his argument, the clear break at v. 6, the lack of a break at v. 14, and the overall progression of the lament from v. 7 through v. 19 argue against his view.

Not only does Lindblom see vv. 15ff. as independent from vv. 1-14, he also insists that the lament in vv. 15-19 does not belong with the rest of the 'Isaiah Apocalypse' at all.[130] The lament reflects a situation of distress, chastisement, and a lack of people. There is an overall sense of hopelessness which, Lindblom maintains, does not accord with the rest of Isa. 24–27. His reasoning is as follows:

1. The composition expresses a general feeling of joy and peace because of the destruction of the city and the blessing of Yahweh (24.14f.; 25.1f.; 26.1f.).
2. It had already been stated in the composition that Yahweh's anger against the people had ceased and the people lived in confidence and hope (26.3f., 12; also 27.2, 4).
3. The present situation is seen as an immediate step into a blissful *eschaton*.
4. The large number of Jews (27.12, 13) gives no reason for such sadness and sorrow.
5. What the poet has before him is not a reduced and languishing people, but a joyful one (27.6).

He concludes:

> Der Gegensatz zwischen dem Inhalt des Klageliedes 26.15-19 und dem Inhalt der übrigen Gedichte der Jesajaapokalypse ist also absolut. Es ist nicht möglich, daß das Klagelied in dieselbe geschichtliche Situation und dieselbe Zeit gehört wie die übrigen Gedichte. Es muß als eine spätere Interpolation beurteilt werden.[131]

Lindblom's assertions require a point-by-point discussion:

1. Lindblom fails to distinguish between the present and the future.[132] He is correct in referring to a sense of joy and peace because of the overthrow of the hostile city and the emergence of the reign of Yahweh, but these events are only announced and anticipated—not yet experienced. The community at present knows chastisement and pain, a reality which harmonizes perfectly with our interpretation of 24.1-20. The destruction of Jerusalem because of the breach of covenant by the people is rightly understood in this national lament as Yahweh's chastisement (v. 16). And the restoration is only a prayer (vv. 16-18); it is not yet a reality.
2. It is true that Yahweh's wrath against his people has passed, but that does not mean that his deliverance has come. In

another context, Second Isaiah announced that Yahweh's wrath against Judah had ended, but it is clear that the deliverance was yet to be realized (40.1, 2).

3. I agree with his third point.
4. The emphasis in the text is not on the number of Jews, but on their present location. As 27.12, 13 states, the Jews are still in exile. That certainly is not a cause for rejoicing.
5. 27.6 speaks of 'coming days'. Once again Lindblom's failure to take seriously the futuristic references has led to misinterpretation.

We conclude that vv. 15-18 are integral to the entire four chapters, and further, that when properly understood, they provide the heart of the lament which originates at v. 7.

2. *Outline of the Lament*

Wildberger's outline is particularly helpful, though I view a number of points differently:

(a) 7: Der grundlegende Glaubenssatz
(b) 8, 9a: Die Sehnsucht nach Gott
(c) 9b, 10: Reflektorisches Zwischenstück
(d) 11: Bitte um Vernichtung der Feinde
(e) 12-15: Gewißheit der Erhörung (mit Rückblick auf Jahwes Treue in der Vergangenheit)
(f) 16-18: Die Klage: Israels Lage ist aussichtslos[133]

I see two major movements leading up to the lament proper in vv. 16-18. First, there is a general statement of belief: when Yahweh enacts his judgments the righteous are rewarded and the wicked are punished (7-10). Second, there is a move from this general perspective to the particular: a plea is made that Yahweh will execute his judgment on behalf of the people in their specific situation of distress with the result that the wicked oppressors will be destroyed (11, 13, 14) and they, the righteous, will be afforded Shalom (12, 15). Then follows the actual lament. My outline looks like this:

1. 7-10: A general statement of belief
2. 11-15: A plea regarding the specific situation
3. 16-18: The lament proper

The major difference between Wildberger's view and my own is with regard to his section 'e'. Rather than viewing vv. 13-15 as a look at past history, I have maintained that the context requires that we take the perfect verbs as precative perfects.[134]

(a) *A General Statement of Belief (vv. 7-10)*

Verse 7 is a statement of trust which functions both as a source of hope for the future and as a reason for the lament in the present. The implication is that if Yahweh indeed makes the paths of life smooth for the righteous, why must this 'righteous nation which keeps faith', continue in its present, desperate state? The appeal to the wisdom tradition (vv. 7-10) reinforces the view that righteous living should be rewarded in this life and thus intensifies the lament.[135]

In vv. 8 and 9a the statement gives rise to a personal expression of hope that Yahweh will begin to execute his judgments in the earth. The *mšpṭym* (judgments) are in parallel with Yahweh's *šm* (name) and *zkr* (memorial). In the OT, the synonymous terms, *šm*, *zkr*, point to Yahweh's acts of deliverance in behalf of his people:

> The name, O Yahweh, is for ever,
> thy renown, O Yahweh, throughout all generations.
> For Yahweh will vindicate his people,
> and have compassion on his servants (Ps. 135.13, 14).[136]

But the judgments of Yahweh mean more than deliverance for the righteous; they imply instruction (*lmd*) for the unrighteous (vv. 9b, 10). The author is affirming an idea that is fundamental to all wisdom teaching, and indeed to the thinking of the ancient Near East, namely, that there is an inherent order in creation to which one must align oneself. If one does what is right, blessings are forthcoming (the way is made level, the path smooth). But if one violates the created order by doing what is wrong, then a curse will follow.[137]

H.H. Schmid points out that when the order is violated, it must be restored, and the Hebrew term for this is *šillem*, 'to make intact', i.e. to restore Shalom.[138] Note that in 26.12 the poet depicts Yahweh's corrective action as the reestablishment of Shalom. W. Kessler conveys the sense of these verses when he notes that the people believed:

> Geschichte nicht ein sinnloses und zufälliges Durcheinander von Machtkämpfen ist, sondern daß ein handelnder, gerechter Wille über und in ihr waltet, der seinem Volk in allen Wirnissen eine ebene Bahn macht.[139]

H. Wildberger cites vv. 9b, 10a with their mention of the 'wicked' and 'the inhabitants of the world' who are able to learn righteousness, as support for his view that 24.5 refers to the ability of all humanity to know God's law. But this connection can not be made for two reasons: (1) As I have indicated, 26.7-10 has to do with the comprehensive created order and humanity's response to it. 24.5, on the other hand, refers to a special people in a special, covenant relationship with Yahweh. The former has to do with natural revelation, while the latter has to do with special revelation. (2) I argued at the beginning of this chapter that the phrase, *whyh bywm hhw'*, in 24.21, introduced a new section of material which closes with the concluding formula, *bywm hhw'*, in 27.1. Therefore, even though this section is not unrelated to 24.1-20, it does have an integrity of its own. Priority ought to be given to the correspondence which exists *within* this section, particularly between vv. 9b, 10 and 25.3. In the latter text the pagan nations observe the *m'śh pl'* of Yahweh and turn to him. This is the same type of thing to which vv. 9b, 10 allude. In neither instance is there a suggestion of a special covenant relationship with Yahweh like we have in 24.5.

Excursus

In recent years it has become common practice to ascribe the rise of apocalyptic thought to a division within the post-exilic Jewish community. The most prolific proponent of this view has been Paul Hanson,[140] who owes a significant debt to O. Plöger and his seminal work, *Theocracy and Eschatology*. Plöger, noting the division within the Jewish community which is reflected in the book of Daniel, sought to trace its historical development through the 'Isaiah-Apocalypse', Trito-Zechariah (12–14) and the book of Joel. The earliest indications of this split are to be found, he maintains, in Isa. 24–27, particularly 26.7-19. Hanson likewise alludes to a division reflected in Isa. 24–27, but follows with the caveat, 'but this hypothesis requires closer examination than can be given here'.[141] Plöger is far less cautious, and it is his work with which we must deal.

Plöger regards the language which contrasts the righteous and the godless (vv. 7-10) as reflecting a 'contemporary' conflict *within* the community. And, in an eschatological passage, the conflict must center around 'eschatological expectations'. The righteous are those who wholeheartedly await the coming of Yahweh, while the godless are those who do not stand firm in the 'eschatological convictions'. Plöger concludes:

> It is clear, then, that we are dealing with a division within the Jewish community. The transgressors... are those who have already fallen prey to this scepticism and who—continuing the line to the Book of Daniel—in times of testing are among those who transgress the covenant of Yahweh.[142]

In my judgment, Plöger's analysis represents a gross distortion of the text. (1) The subsequent verses (11-18), which convey a plea for the destruction of the enemy and the restoration of the Jewish community, clearly demonstrate that the dichotomy established between the righteous and the godless in vv. 7-10 must be understood as a contrast between the enemy (the godless) and the Jewish community (the righteous), rather than as an indication of a conflict within the community. The general statements prepare for the specific request. (2) There is no hint in the context of tension within the community. Verse 8 is in the first person plural, suggesting that the entire community is of one mind. Later, the nation (v. 15) is spoken of as a homogeneous group, and the national resurrection announced in v. 19 gives no intimation of a separate resurrection like that found in Daniel 12. (3) The 'traditional language... from the Psalms and Wisdom literature', simply cannot be construed to bear the weight of the eschatological expectations which Plöger places on it. There is insufficient evidence for interpreting the phrase, 'the way of the righteous', as 'the path of the man who is righteous because the goal of his journey is the eschatological millennium'; or that the disobedience of the godless is to be viewed 'in the sense of doubting or not paying attention to eschatological conviction'.[143]

In summary, there is no evidence in this communal lament for a 'contemporary conflict' or tension within the community. This document reflects a single-minded will to be freed from the oppressors, and for Israel to be restored to its earlier glory. While it is certainly true that the internal conflict which is evidenced in the book of Daniel had a history, one must look elsewhere than Isaiah 26 for its origination.

(b) *A Plea Regarding the Specific Situation (vv. 11-15)*

With v. 11 the author makes the transition from the general to the particular. The unrighteous are now identified as the antagonists of the people and as Yahweh's enemies. We may assume that the raised hand of Yahweh in this context refers to the overthrow of the enemy which had been promised in 24.21, 22; 25.2; 26.5, 6, an action which still lies in the future, as this verse confirms.[144]

Verse 12 is a request to Yahweh to create a state of Shalom for his people. And the juxtaposition of v. 12 with v. 11 suggests that the prophet believed that the destruction of the enemy would result in the well-being of Israel.[145]

The prophet reasons that the time is right for Yahweh to create Shalom for his people because (*kî*) Yahweh has by now adequately avenged Judah's wrongs (v. 12b, which presumably is a reference to the exile). While v. 12b may also be rendered: 'You have accomplished all our works for us' (cf. RSV, and others), support for our proposed rendering ('Since you have also requited all our misdeeds') is four-fold: (1) Textual: We noted above that the only unambiguous reading among the versions was the Targum which made reference to 'our transgressions'.[146] (2) Internal: Wildberger correctly notes the word-play between *p'lt* and *b'lwnw*: 'Das Handeln Jahwes (*p'l*) war durch das Herrschen (*b'l*) der Herren herausgefordert'.[147] Certainly it must be recognized that normally when Yahweh's actions toward his people are executed by means of other nations, the action is corrective in nature. (3) Structural: I see an A B A′ B′ arrangement in the text which connects v. 12 with v. 16, which is a clear reference to Yahweh's chastisement of his people:

A —v. 11	B —v. 12
A′—vv. 13, 14	B′—vv. 15, 16

Verses 11 & 12 specify two groups: the enemy (A) and Judah (B). Verse 13 gives greater focus to the enemy (they are the ones who have been ruling over Judah), while v. 14, as a request for the enemy's destruction is a reiteration of v. 11. Verse 15 gives concrete expression to the request for Shalom in v. 12a (Shalom = national well-being), while v. 16 picks up on the notion of retribution in v. 12b. The request for Shalom is justified because Yahweh's correctional action has already taken place (cf. 40.1, 2). (4) Contextual: The lament (vv. 7-19) clearly reflects a situation of distress, which, according to standard prophetic thinking, was the result of disobedience. This understanding is confirmed by the mention of Yahweh's *chastisement* of the people in v. 16. Finally, this view is in harmony with the greater context, namely 24.1-20, which we have interpreted as the depiction of the destruction of Jerusalem and the ensuing exile, both of which were the result of the disobedience of the people of Judah.

Generally, interpreters view vv. 13-15 as a brief review of the history of Israel: vv. 13, 14 refer to the period of the judges and Yahweh's deliverance, and v. 15 alludes to the periods of Israel's greatness under David and Solomon.[148] But I disagree with this interpretation for the following reasons: (1) In v. 13b priority is given to the *present*: 'we acknowledge your name alone'. It would make little sense to contrast the dominion of various Canaanite rulers in the far distant period of the judges with the prophet's claim of faithfulness to Yahweh in the present. Rather, the sense of the verse is this: 'Despite the domination of those who are currently ruling over us, we remain faithful to you alone, O Yahweh'. (2) The A B A′ B′ relationship we noted above suggests a parallelism of tense as well as of subject.[149] (3) Rendering vv. 13-15 in a precative sense harmonizes much better with the sense of desperation and hopeless-ness that is reflected in vv. 16-18. Instead of creating a historical diversion, the prophet continues to plead with Yahweh to reverse the devastating situation in which the prophet and people find themselves.

Verse 13 mentions other masters, *'dnym*. While this term often suggests other deities, such a rendering here would leave no antecedent for 'them' in v. 14b. It is possible to regard *'dnym* as human rulers, and given the mixture of politics and religion in the ancient (and modern) Near East, one should see in *'dnym* a comprehensive term which includes both the human rulers and their deities.[150] The function of the verse is to highlight the faithfulness of the people in the midst of a lamentable situation of foreign domination.[151]

Verse 14. The finality of death was recognized in the ancient Near East.[152] In my view there are two different ways to interpret this verse: (1) The author may have been alluding to the seemingly inevitable fate of his people: 'We will not live if this oppression continues. There will be no restoration, and as a people we will be lost forever, therefore destroy our oppressors before it is too late'. Support for this understanding may be found in the fact that v. 19, an affirmation of national restoration, stands as a direct response to v. 14.[153] On the other hand, it may be argued that the immediate context which focuses on the enemy favors a different interpretation: (2) 'Since the fate of the dead is irreversible, bring that fate upon our enemies'. The parallelism between 14a and 14b supports this rendering.

We argued above for the integrity of the section 24.21–27.1. Therefore one may expect a correspondence of ideas and language *within* this section. The verb, *pqdt*, in v. 14, 'May you attack and destroy them', calls to mind the opening verse in this section, 'On that day Yahweh will punish (attack) the host of the height'. This mythological phrase was then given historical specificity in the announcement of the coming destruction of the city in 25.2 (and again in 26.5, 6). The connection of the lament (26.7-19) with the prophecy against the hostile city serves to link the enemy in 26.11, 13, 14 with the wicked city, and thus with the opening announcement of the destruction of the hostile powers in 24.21. I have suggested that the city is Babylon. The lament, I maintain, was written during the exile while Judah suffered under the oppression of her Babylonian overlords.

Verse 15 is a plea for the increase of both the people and their land. As such it is a request for the reversal of the situation described in 24.1-20, particularly 24.6, 'and few men are left', and 24.11 'the joy of earth has gone into exile'. We note further that the Targum of Isaiah interprets v. 15 as a reference to the exile: *'p 'tyk 't lqrb' glwt hwn*, 'Yes, you are about to bring near (home) their exiles'.

(c) *The Lament Proper (vv. 16-18)*

Judah's present situation is acknowledged to be the result of Yahweh's chastening,[154] and the hopelessness which the people feel is communicated in the imagery of a woman who endures the agony of childbearing, and yet brings forth nothing: Judah's attempts at restoration from the exile have been in vain.[155]

The imagery of childbirth as a symbol relating to the exile is well known in the Isaianic tradition. In addition to the pericope in 26.17, 18, there are three other pericopae which employ this imagery. First, the prophet known as Second Isaiah announced to the exiles that in a short time, when the exile has ended, they will say,

> 'Who has borne me these?
> I was bereaved and barren,
> exiled and put away,
> but who has brought up these?
> Behold, I was left alone;
> whence then have these come?' (49.21).

Second, we read,

'Sing, O barren one, who did not bear;
break forth into singing and cry aloud,
you who have not been in travail!
For the children of the desolate one will be more
than the children of her that is married',
says the Lord (54.1).

The third pericope comes from Third Isaiah and is of special significance,

Before she was in labor she gave birth,
before her pain came upon her
she was delivered a son.
Who has heard such a thing?
Who has seen such a thing?
Shall a land be born in one day?
Shall a nation be brought forth in one moment?
For as soon as Zion was in labor
she brought forth her sons (66.7, 8).

This passage refers to the return of the exiles, an event which has taken place. Westermann comments with reference to this pericope, 'The land of Judah has her children all of a sudden restored to her', and he dates it shortly after the first return in 538.[156]

In my judgment, it is important to interpret all four of the Isaianic birth passages with an eye to seeing the interrelationship among them. Westermann, with most scholars, notes a connection between Isaiah 66 and Second Isaiah: 'the basis (of 66.7, 8) is the proclamation of Deutero-Isaiah (49.20-23)'.[157] And recently more and more scholars have argued for a close relationship between Second Isaiah and Isa. 24–27.[158] In the light of the interrelationship involved in these three different portions of the Isaianic tradition, two points emerge: (1) In Isa. 49.21; 54.1 and 66.7, 8, the birth imagery functions to symbolize Judah's exile and return. We may reasonably assume that for the other passage in this tradition (26.17, 18) the function of the imagery is identical. (2) It would be incongruous for the anouncement that the birth has already taken place (66.7, 8) to antedate the lament that all hope for 'childbirth' seemed lost (26.17, 18). It follows that Isa. 26.17, 18, and most, if not all of Isa. 24–27, was written prior to Isaiah 66 and the first return of 538.

3. *The Heilsorakel*

The precise translation, determination of the speaker, and the assignment of genre for v. 19 are all very complex issues. For the multitudinous possibilities see Kaiser's extended and helpful discussion.[159] For my part I regard the verse as a *Heilsorakel* spoken by Yahweh, a position which has found general agreement.[160] I find support also in Westermann's investigation of the lament of the people. Generally, such a lament will close with a vow of praise, but often, particularly in the prophetic literature, an answer from God is given instead, precisely as we have here.[161] Further, this form-critical observation argues against those who wish to see v. 19 as a later interpolation. For this reason, Wildberger correctly insists:

> Wesentlich ist aber, daß 19 streng im Blick auf das Vorhergehende interpretiert wird. So oder so ist der Vers als das große Dennoch gegenüber 17f. zu verstehen, und auf keinen Fall darf mit der Schere der Literarkritik auseinandergeschnitten werden, was formgeschichtlich zusammengehört.[162]

In my judgment there can be no doubt that v. 19 refers to a *national* rather than an individual resurrection. This view is supported by (1) the greater context: a situation of exile (cf. our discussion of 24.1-20 and *passim*); (2) the date: as I indicated above there has been an emerging consensus that Isa. 24–27 is to be dated close to the time of the exile; and most importantly, (3) the immediate context: a *national* lament which (a) refers to Yahweh's people *en masse* over against the enemy (v. 11), (b) affirms the faithfulness of the entire people during the period of foreign oppression (v. 13), (c) depicts Shalom in terms of national well-being (v. 15), (d) notes Yahweh's chastisement of the people as a whole rather than individuals within the society (v. 16), (e) employs the language of childbirth, an image well known in the Isaianic tradition as connoting national exile and restoration (vv. 17, 18a), and (f) thinks of deliverance as the repopulation of the land (v. 18b, c). All of this is a prelude to the announcement of national restoration. The message of 26.19 is the same as that of Ezekiel 37, despite the arbitrary claim of Rudolph to the contrary: 'Daß hier wie in Ez. 37 ein Bild für die Heimkehr aus dem Exil vorliege ist durch die gewählten Ausdrücke ausgeschlossen'.[163]

But still the question remains: Why does the author choose the particular imagery of resurrection to announce the return of the exiles? Two reasons suggest themselves:

(1) Within the Isaianic tradition the exile was associated with death. I cite the following: (a) 5.13, 14:

> Therefore my people go into exile for want of knowledge;
> their honored men are dying of hunger . . .
> Therefore Sheol has enlarged its appetite and opened its mouth
> beyond measure, and the nobility of Jerusalem and her multitude
> go down, her throng and he who exults in her.

(b) Note also 28.15. (c) It is possible to see Isa. 29.1-4 as an original Isaianic oracle of judgment against Jerusalem which would have been seen in the aftermath of 587 as a prophecy of Jerusalem's destruction. Verse 4 suggests the realm of the dead. Note the double use of *'pr* which would correspond with *škny 'pr* in 26.19. (d) While the imagery in 52.2 ('Shake yourself from the dust, arise, O captive, Jerusalem',) is of a captive, humbled and forced to sit on the ground, rather than a dead person, the presence of *qwm* and *'pr* in both pericopae may suggest a finely nuanced correlation. (e) Certainly the images of barrenness which we mentioned above (49.21; 54.1, 2) suggest lifelessness.[164] This survey of the Isaianic tradition suggests that the author of Isa. 24–27 may have been relating to a particular understanding of the exile which saw it as the death of the nation.

(2) The explanation for the resurrection language may lie in the inherent meaning of the exile itself. J.Z. Smith has stated this well: 'To be exiled is to be in a state of chaos, decreation, and death; to return from exile is to be re-created and reborn'.[165] I have stated above that in 24.1-20 the author wrote of the destruction of the land of Judah and its people. He limned this devastation in the imagery of the chaos myth. But that was not the final word. As soon as this Stygian scene closes we hear that Yahweh is about to ascend his throne as king and overthrow the enemy forces which have temporarily overcome his people. As in primeval time when Yahweh created life out of chaos, so now Yahweh, the king, will re-create life out of the chaos of the exile. The finality of the destruction required the originality of a new creation, a resurrection.[166]

G. *The Defeat of the Hostile Powers Restated (26.20–27.1)*

The national restoration is predicated on the destruction of the enemy which is the subject of 26.20–27.1. While several interpreters maintain that v. 20 refers to the tradition about the Flood, I see it as an allusion to the Exodus tradition (particularly Exodus 12).[167] Support for my position is provided by (1) the context and (2) a lexical study of the verse itself.

(1) The context. We noted above that this section began with a reference to the Exodus tradition: *'śyt pl'* (25.1), a phrase which was employed in the hymn of praise to Yahweh for the act of deliverance which would soon be performed. The more immediate context is reminiscent of Israel's bondage in Egypt. Note the following parallels: (a) the oppressive, foreign domination (26.11, 13; Exod. 1.8-14); (b) the intense lament (26.7-18; Exod. 2.23); (c) Yahweh's response promising deliverance from the enemy (26.19; Exod. 3.7-8). Not one of these three elements finds a parallel in the flood story.

(2) There are several points in v. 20 which suggest that reference is being made to the Exodus tradition. (a) The notion of hiding behind closed doors while Yahweh executes his destructive work against the enemy calls to mind Exodus 12, especially 12.23:

> For the Lord will pass through to slay the Egyptians, and when he sees the blood on the lintel and on the two door posts, the Lord will pass over the door, and will not allow the destroyer to enter your houses to slay you.

(b) The use of the root *'rb* alludes to the tradition of Yahweh passing over his own people while smiting the Egyptians. (c) The phrase *m'ṭ rq'* 'in a little while', which implies that the deliverance is imminent, finds a parallel in Exod. 12.11:

> In this manner you shall eat it: your loins girded, your sandals on your feet, and your staff in your hand; and you shall eat it *in haste* (emphasis mine).

(d) Finally, *ḥdr* signifies the rooms of a house,[168] which accords with the Exodus tradition.

To be sure, the reference to 'shutting the doors' might be construed as a reference to Gen. 7.16 as Wildberger and others have attempted to do,[169] but there are several points of dissimilarity between 26.20 and the flood story which militate against a typological correspondence. There is not the same sense of urgency in the flood story as is evidenced in 26.20. It was only after Noah had been in the ark seven days that the 'waters of the flood came upon the earth' (Gen. 7.10). The major motifs of the two stories are also different. The theme of Isa. 26.20 is the defeat of the enemy oppressors and the deliverance of the people of Yahweh, while the point of the flood story is the preservation of a remnant from the universal destruction.

There is one major issue in v. 21 that demands attention: who are the *yšb h'rṣ* that Yahweh is about to punish? Most interpreters view this in the light of 24.5 and interpret it as a reference to the judgment of all humanity. Further, they cite the mention of *dmyh* as support, since they view this term as an allusion to one of the 'stipulations' in the Noachic covenant (Gen. 9.6). They do this despite the fact that, for the most part, they deny any unity to the composition.

I regard this argumentation for connecting 26.21 with 24.5 as unconvincing, and maintain that v. 21 refers to 24.21ff. for the following reasons:

(1) I demonstrated above (section A.1. of this chapter) that the phrase *whyh bywm hhw'*, in 24.21, introduced a new section in the composition. The various parts of this section should be interpreted *primarily within* the context of this section, rather than by appealing to the previous section of the composition. Further, the use of *pgd*, along with the reference to Israel's enemies in 26.21, forms an appropriate *inclusio* with 24.21. The destruction of the enemy is announced both at the beginning and the end of this section.

(2) It is not necessary that the phrase *yšb h'rṣ* refer to the same entity each time it is used. On at least one other occasion the author used one phrase to refer to opposite entities: in 26.9 the phrase, *yšby tbl* alluded to Judah's enemy, while in 26.18 it referred to Judah's own offspring. If within the *same pericope* one phrase may be employed to indicate two different groups of people, then surely we must allow that same flexibility of meaning for a phrase that occurs in two *separate sections* of a composition. Precise meanings for such phrases must be determined by context rather than simple cross-referencing.

(3) I have shown in the previous chapter that there is no correlation between the use of *dm* here and *bryt 'wlm* in 24.5. The context suggests that the bloodshed mentioned in 26.21 refers to the slain of Israel. Parallels may be found in three passages: (a) Ps. 79.3, 10 which is a communal lament beseeching Yahweh to avenge 'the outpoured blood of thy servants'. (b) Deut. 32.43. The entire pattern of Deuteronomy 32 is similar to that of Isa. 24–27: After announcing his judgment on Israel (vv. 19-33), Yahweh promises to have compassion on his people (v. 36). Then he will take vengeance on his enemies (vv. 41, 42) in order to avenge the blood of his servants:

> Praise his people, O you nations,
> For he avenges the blood of his servants,
> And takes vengeance on his adversaries,
> and makes expiation for the land of his people (Deut. 32.43).

(c) Finally, I note Jer. 51.35. In the oracle of judgment against Babylon, fallen Jerusalem is portrayed as saying, 'My blood be upon the inhabitants of Chaldea'.

Isa. 27.1 brings to a conclusion the section celebrating the imminent victory of Yahweh over the enemy.[170] While the enemy is now portrayed mythologically as the chaos monster, our exegesis has shown that there is no question but that the monster functions simply as the representation of the historical enemy, much like it does in 51.9-11. The moorings with history have not been cut off, as is the case in the later apocalyptic literature.[171]

DeVries makes note of the several occurrences of the phrase *bywm hhw'*, which function as 'concluding formulae'.[172] As such, these formulae tend toward 'epitomization', which he defines as 'the product and process of succinct, formal summarization; particularly through authoritative interpretation in narrative conclusion'.[173] DeVries' understanding of 27.1 fits well with our analysis of 24.21–27.1. Not only does 27.1 reiterate the motif expressed in the opening verses of this section (24.21, 22), but it also summarizes the theme that has been repeated throughout: Yahweh will defeat the enemy. In the light of the fact that the author understood the exile as a collapse into chaos, it is appropriate that he interpret the termination of the exile as the destruction of the chaos monster.

Chapter 4

THE REUNIFICATION OF ISRAEL (ISAIAH 27.2-13)

A. *The Vineyard Song Revisited (27.2-6)*

1. *The Determination of the Unit*

There is universal agreement that the next unit is modeled on the song of the vineyard in Isa. 5.1-7. But there is disagreement as to where the unit ends. Gray, Kissane, March, and Holladay terminate it at v. 6.[1] Lohmann, Duhm, Delitzsch, Wildberger, Kaiser, and Redditt mark the end at v. 5.[2] Surprisingly, Lindblom extends the unit through v. 11.[3]

For everyone, except Lindblom, the question of the proper *terminus ad quem* centers on the function of v. 6. Of these who end the song at v. 5, Wildberger connects v. 6 with the following verses (6-11); Delitzsch and Redditt make it a one-verse pericope, and Duhm excludes it from the song and the 'Apocalypse' altogether.

There are four points which militate against the view of Wildberger (and Lindblom): (1) The dramatic change in subject matter from the vineyard and Yahweh's protection of it, to mention of the slaying of peoples and Yahweh's contention with them; (2) the shift from a future perspective in vv. 2-6 to the past in v. 7; (3) the use of the interrogative which often marks a new beginning; (4) the fact that Isa. 5.1-7 serves as a model for 27.2ff., which suggests that the two songs end in a similar fashion.

The introductory *hb'ym* in v. 6 suggests a break after v. 5, but the subject matter of the vine indicates continuity. In my view, Kaiser's designation of v. 6 as a 'postscript to the song',[4] is the most appropriate proposal in that it reflects both the continuity and discontinuity of the text.

2. *The Perspective of the Song*

We noted the oddity of Lindblom's proposal of delimiting the unit as

vv. 2-11. Lindblom errs methodologically in that he insists on eliminating the introductory formula, *bywm hhw'*, or its equivalent, each time it occurs. 'Wir müssen vorläufig von den einleitenden Worten, *bywm hhw'*, mit ihrer Zeitbestimmung absehen und das Gedicht für sich untersuchen'.[5] But if we are to interpret the text which has been preserved for us, then this line of reasoning is unacceptable.

The elimination of the introductory *bywm hhw'* has further led Lindblom, Rudolph, Procksch, and Plöger to conclude that vv. 2-6 are not eschatological in nature.[6] But, as we have noted, such a conclusion is based on a hypothetical text. When the phrase is retained and the text kept intact, it is clear that the author is looking to the future day when Yahweh will have come from his place (26.20) and will have destroyed Judah's enemies. It is that glorious day in the future when Yahweh will have inaugurated his uninhibited reign. This is a view which looks ahead to the restoration of the vineyard which is the whole house of Israel (cf. 5.7a).

3. *The Relationship of vv. 2-6 to 5.1-7*

The points of contact between the original vineyard song and 27.2-6 are numerous and have been cited often:[7] (a) Both pericopae are songs. (b) Both refer to the fertility of the vineyard [*bqrn bn šmn*—5.1, *krm ḥmr*—27.2]. (c) In the original song the vineyard's betrayal of Yahweh's care leads to Yahweh's wrath (5.5, 6), while in 27.4 Yahweh has no wrath. (d) Briars and thorns are encouraged by Yahweh to overtake the vineyard in 5.6, but they will be burned up if they appear in the vineyard in 27.4. (e) While Yahweh forbids the rain to water his unfaithful vineyard (5.6), he takes it upon himself to water the restored vineyard regularly in 27.3. (f) Yahweh will bring evil upon the wayward vineyard (5.5, 6), but the future vineyard he will guard night and day lest any evil come upon it (27.3). (g) While the yield of the original vineyard was malevolent (5.7), the restored vineyard will prove beneficial to the entire world (27.6).

Clearly the emphasis is given to the element of contrast. This suggests that the purpose of the second vineyard song is to announce that the judgment which was prophesied in the original song will soon come to an end. The time of wrath is past and the day of Yahweh's epiphany to deliver and restore his people is at hand.

We know from Isa. 5.7 that the vineyard is the *whole* house of Israel. If we are to follow consistently the typological correspondence between the two songs, then we must assume that the writer was referring to both the erstwhile Northern kingdom and Judah. There is here a hint of the reunification theme which is sounded in vv. 12, 13. National restoration implies national reunification.

Verses 4b and 5 convey a veiled invitation to the North, albeit in the guise of a warning. Until recently scholars had agreed that vv. 4b, 5 referred to any external threat to the security of the Jewish community.[8] As Kaiser notes, the warlike imagery and the making of peace (cf. Josh. 9.15) argue in favor of this view.[9] In recent years, however, Kessler and Wildberger have maintained that the cryptic phrase, *yḥzq bm'wzy*, is an allusion to the asylum of the temple (1 Kgs 1.51; 2.28), and the enemy from within would be the Samaritans. According to this view, v. 5 would be an invitation to the Samaritans, who had built their own altar on Mt Gerizim, to return to Jerusalem and make peace with Yahweh.[10]

There is much to be said for this proposal: (1) Since the vineyard song celebrates the restoration of all Israel, and since everything else in the composition has only made mention of Judah, it is logical to expect that attention be given to the inclusion of the North. (2) The following verse (v. 6) with its mention of Jacob/Israel appears to be a reference to the North.[11] (3) We know from other prophets of the exile that their vision of national restoration included the idea of the reunification of the two divided kingdoms (Jer. 31.1-9, 15-22; Ezek. 37.15-23). Note the wording in Jer. 31.6, which seems to parallel the sentiments of 27.5:

> For there shall be a day when watchmen will call
> in the hill country of Ephraim:
> 'Arise, and let us go up to Zion,
> to the Lord our God'.

This third point leads me to suggest a correction of the view proposed by Kessler and Wildberger. Since the theme of the reunification of Israel was well known in the exilic period there is good reason to date this *parallel* pericope in the corresponding period, rather than later during the time of the Samaritan schism.[12] Indeed, the schism would all but preclude the note of reconciliation that is struck in these verses.

B. *A Lesson from Israel's Tragic History (27.7-11)*

1. *A Summary of the Difficulties*

We come now to vv. 7-11, a section which is considered by all interpreters to be the most difficult of the entire four chapters.[13] The problems are numerous. (1) The identity of the parties in all the verses except v. 9 is not immediately apparent. (2) There is a frequent and seemingly inexplicable change in tense between the perfect and the imperfect. (3) One would expect v. 8 to be an elaboration on v. 7, but the shift from masculine to feminine suffixes becomes problematic. This has led some scholars to associate v. 8 with v. 10. Duhm alleges that v. 8 is from a third hand and was written in the margin alongside v. 10, and only later taken into the text at its present location.[14] (4) The change from *bz't* to *wzh* is an odd change from masculine to feminine. (5) The connection between v. 9 and v. 10 is less than obvious. This has led Kissane and Rudolph to place v. 9 after v. 11.[15] Clearly the would-be interpreter is faced with a formidable task.

2. *A Proposed Solution*

These editorially related difficulties are in no small measure responsible for the lack of consensus as to the meaning of this section, and more particularly, the identity of the city in v. 10. The views on the latter topic range from a foreign city,[16] to Samaria,[17] to Jerusalem.[18] There has seemed so little evidence on which one could base a position with confidence.[19] But recently, the French scholar J. Vermeylen has argued forcefully for a lexical correspondence between 27.7-11 and Isa. 17.2-11. This would indicate that the later writer was reworking the earlier material in a new context in order to say something about the erstwhile Northern kingdom and its capital, Samaria.[20] I would add that the writer of 27.7-11 is also dependent on Hosea's announcement of judgment against the Northern kingdom, and a few other Isaianic passages. Note the following references:

(1) 27.7. *mkhw*, Isa. 9.12, 10.20 (*mkhw*, *mkhw*). The former passage from First Isaiah is a reference to Yahweh who smote Israel, while the latter refers to Assyria as the one who smote Israel. Note also Hos. 9.16 (*hkh*).

(2) 27.8. The phrase, *qdym... hgh*, seems to be taken from Hos. 13.15 and 12.2; both are metaphorical allusions to Assyria. And Yahweh's *rîb* with Israel was well known from Hosea's oracle in 4.1.

(3) 27.9. The three items, *mzbḥ*, *'šrym*, *ḥmnym*, as symbols of *Jacob's* apostasy in v. 9 find a clear correspondence in Isa. 17.8[21] (cf. Hos. 10.2).

(4) 27.10. *wn'zb*; the cities of Israel will be forsaken (*k'zwbt*, *'zbw*—17.9). Note also *s'p* in 17.6.

(5) 27.11. *qṣyrh*; cf. 17.5, 11. The telling phrase, *l' 'm bynwt*, is reminiscent of Hosea's similar indictment of his people: *w'm l' ybyn* (4.14). Note also Isa. 1.3; 6.9, 10 which refer to both Judah's and Israel's lack of understanding. Yahweh's judgment to withhold grace (*l' yrḥmnw*) in 27.11 is related to the judgment in Isa. 9.16, *l' yrḥm*, but particularly to the symbolic name given to Hosea's child, *l' rḥmh* (Hos. 1.6). Finally, *'šhw*, as a reference to Yahweh, is taken from Isa. 17.7 (cf. also Hos. 8.14).

It is necessary now to apply this lexical study to a more detailed analysis of the text. Verse 7 contrasts the fates of two different groups of people, both of which have been the object of Yahweh's wrath.[22] The context, namely vv. 6 and 9 which mention Jacob/Israel specifically, suggests that the one nation which has been slain is Israel. In the light of the reference in 10.20:

> In that day the remnant of Israel and the survivors of the house of Jacob will no more lean upon him that smote them (*mkhw*)

it seems clear that this is a reference to the Assyrians' capture of the Northern kingdom and destruction of Samaria in 722. This view is supported by v. 8, which employs the image of the *east wind*, a well-known metaphor for Assyria.[23]

Note also that the word *trybnh* implies a covenant relationship, and that the word *šlḥh* is often indicative of a close relationship which has been terminated.[24]

On the surface, v. 9 appears to be a non sequitur: any logical connection between it and the preceding verse is less than obvious. Most interpreters agree that *bz't* points to the following material and implies a condition which must be met.[25] Accordingly we must assume that Jacob, rather than Yahweh, is the subject of *bśwmw*. It is Jacob who must destroy the altar and the *asherim* and incense altars.[26] Here there is little doubt that the author is dependent on 17.8.

Verse 10 resumes the motif of judgment that we noted in v. 8. The city whose population was cast forth (*šlḥh*) now lies in ruins, deserted (*n'zb*) and forsaken, as it had been prophesied in 17.9. The reason for the judgment is stated in v. 11: Because this is a people without understanding, Yahweh will have no compassion on them. Note the similar causal relationship between Israel's lack of knowledge (4.1, 14) and Yahweh's judgment of no compassion as symbolized in the name of Hosea's daughter, *l' rḥmh* (Hos. 1.6), and actualized in the destruction brought by Assyria.

In my judgment, the force of this lexical study cannot be denied. Clearly vv. 7-11 are dealing with the fate of the erstwhile Northern kingdom, and the city of Samaria. But lest we conclude prematurely that this is *all* that this pericope is concerned with, due consideration must be given to other evidence—evidence which might suggest that the pericope is dealing with the devastation of Jerusalem in 587 as well. Note the following study of terms:

1. While it is true that the antecedent for *mkhw* is properly to be found in 10.20, a reference to the Assyrians, this is not the case with *hrg* in the second half of v. 7. Rather, we note that a form of *hrg* is employed to depict Yahweh's destruction of Jerusalem in Lam. 2.4, 21; 3.43; Jer. 4.31.
2. *šlḥh*. This term is used elsewhere with reference to the exile of Judah to Babylon (Isa. 50.1; Jer. 24.5; 29.20).
3. *qdym*. Babylon as well as Assyria may be alluded to with this term (cf. Jer. 18.17; Ezek. 17.10; 19.12).
4. It is possible that the term, 'Jacob', which in the exilic period is often used interchangeably with 'Israel' and 'Judah' to refer to the exiled people of Judah,[27] now refers to the entire 'house of Israel', and that 17.8 has been re-interpreted to apply to this broader community.
5. *bṣwrh*. Clearly many cities in the OT are referred to as *bṣwrh*, but Ezek. 21.25 (20) mentions Jerusalem specifically as 'Jerusalem the fortified'. It is a passage which highlights the irony of an inaccessible Jerusalem being reduced to ruins (by Babylon).
6. *bdd*. Obviously, any destroyed city would be alone (*bdd*), but no other city is so portrayed in the entire Hebrew Bible.[28] Rather, one immediately thinks of the opening lament over fallen Jerusalem in the book of Lamentations: 'How lonely (*bdd*) sits the city'.
7. Isa. 32.14, 15, as a prophecy of the destruction of Jerusalem, may provide the backdrop for this description in v. 10. Note the use of *'zb* and *mdbr* in both pericopae.

8. The unexpected mention of women in v. 11a may have been intended as an allusion to the fulfillment of the prophecy against the haughty daughters of Zion in 3.16–4.1.
9. The terminology in v.11b (except the phrase *l' yrḥmnw*) could apply to Judah as easily as it could to Israel in the north.

The lexical support for viewing the referent in this pericope as Judah/Jerusalem is significant. But, as we indicated above, so is the support for viewing the referent as Israel/Samaria. If we take seriously the context, namely, the restoration of the *whole house* of Israel, then we ought to view the duplicity of referents as the result of a *conflation* of two traditions: one relating to the fall of the Northern kingdom and the other to the fall of Judah. The author, who has created an inclusive context with the restored vineyard, Israel, in vv. 2-6, and the idealized Davidic kingdom in v. 12,[29] has attempted in the intervening verses to bring together the two separate traditions which depict the termination of the two parts of that kingdom.

We noted above the numerous, editorially related problems in vv. 7-11. Many scholars see these as evidence of corruption of the text. I propose that they are the result of poor editing when the two separate traditions were conflated. The traditions associated with the Northern kingdom are conveyed consistently in the masculine form (vv. 7, 9), while those which are related to Judah/Jerusalem are in the feminine (vv. 8, 10). This is a possible explanation for the otherwise inexplicable alternation between the masculine and feminine in these verses. Perhaps, too, this view helps to explain the awkward transitions between verses: *lkn*, v. 9; *kî*, v. 10; and the lack of any transition at all between vv. 7 and 8.

3. *The Purpose of the Pericope*

The section, vv. 7-11, serves as both a plea and a warning. The plea is that the people will renounce all forms of idolatry (v. 9). While the author states that this renunciation is necessary for the expiation of sins, the context suggests that his ultimate concern is the restoration of the vineyard and the reunification of Israel, which cannot be effected until all apostasy is terminated. Note the similar logic in the parallel passage in Ezek. 37.15-23 (see especially v. 23).

The warning is accomplished through a backward look. Yahweh, who previously had unleashed his judgment on the insubordinate vineyard (vv. 7, 8, 10), will not refrain from executing his wrath in the future if this people fails to acknowledge Him as the true God (v. 11).[30]

4. *The Date of 27.7-11*

Kessler proposed that this pericope refers to the destruction of Samaria in 296, and was added to the larger composition subsequent to this date.[31] But Wildberger wisely cautions against this view because the information regarding the destruction of Samaria during this period is both inadequate and uncertain.[32] He locates the pericope in the Persian epoch, 'perhaps in the time of Nehemiah', and designates it a prophecy of the fall of Samaria. The emphasis on the *harsh* judgment would be due to the fact that Samaria was a 'bone of contention' (*Zankapfel*) during this time. The fact that we know nothing of the destruction of Samaria during this period only indicates that we are dealing with an unfulfilled prophecy.[33]

In my view, there is one major problem with Wildberger's proposal. The context carries the theme of reunification; the tone is conciliatory in vv. 2-6 and 12, 13. A *prediction* of destruction would be inconsistent with the author's appeal to the people of the North. How could the author exhort the people to make peace with Yahweh (v. 5) on the one hand, and announce their imminent devastation on the other?

While Plöger does not regard this passage as a prediction of Samaria's destruction, he does place it in the Persian period, with Wildberger. Recognizing the inherent problem of locating a pericope whose theme is the reunification of Israel in a period which was characterized by extreme tensions between the two houses of Israel, Plöger appeals to an imaginary group within Israel. These people who were responsible for the 'hopes expressed in ch. xxvii', were not a part of the 'exclusively Jerusalemite circles, such as were represented by Nehemiah, for instance, but by people who . . . (had) not lost faith in a restoration of ancient Israel'.[34] While this view is possible, it is also possible that such a group is simply the figment of Plöger's imagination.

In my judgment, there is no reason to date these verses in the time of Nehemiah. Rather, I maintain that they belong to the exilic or earlier post-exilic era for the following reasons:

1. We have maintained that the rest of the composition should be dated no later than the days of the exile. Yahweh's deliverance of his people from the chaos of exile is only

anticipated, not yet realized. While it is possible that vv. 7-11 are a much later addition, there is no compelling evidence that would require this view.

2. The hopes for reunification ran high toward the end of the exile as evidenced by the two passages which parallel 27.7-11: Jer. 31.1-8, 15-22; and Ezek. 37.15-23. Clearly, the most congenial context for our pericope is the same one which produced Jeremiah 31 and Ezekiel 37.
3. Related to (2) is the fact that in both of the parallel passages there is a word of warning which accompanies the appeal to the North: In Jer. 31.18-22 Ephraim is exhorted to learn from the chastening action of Yahweh and return to Him. Similarly, Ezek. 37.23 functions as a warning against further idolatry.[35] It seems to me that 27.7-11 conveys a similar tone of admonition. Verses 7, 8 recall Yahweh's past chastisement of his people, as do vv. 10, 11a. An appeal to forsake all forms of idolatry is made in v. 9. Finally, v. 11b is a warning that Yahweh's grace will not be extended automatically. Indeed, if the true knowledge of Yahweh is rejected, God will not have compassion on them.
4. In the lexical study above (pp. 90f.), I noted several words which are generally associated with the tradition of the destruction of Jerusalem.[36] It is obvious, though nonetheless significant for the dating of this pericope, that these are exilic terms, appearing in the exilic books, Jeremiah, Lamentations, Ezekiel, and Second Isaiah. While this observation does not prove conclusively that the pericope itself is from the period of the exile, it certainly lends support to such a notion.

C. *The Return of the Exiles (27.12, 13)*

1. *Harvest Rather Than Judgment (v. 12)*

There is little disagreement that the scope envisioned in v. 12 includes the idealized borders of the Davidic kingdom. But there is a significant divergence of opinion regarding the meaning of this verse. Duhm, Kaiser, Gray and Wildberger interpret the harvest motif as a judgment of separation: separating the wheat (Jews) from the chaff (Gentiles).[37] But interestingly, Kaiser remarks that, 'We are not told what happens to the gentiles'.[38] He is absolutely correct. In fact, there is no mention of Gentiles (or chaff) in the text. This is a view which has been interpolated by the commentators who mistakenly maintain that *ḥbṭ* and *lqṭ* connote a metaphorical separation of the wheat from the chaff. In the majority of the occurrences of *ḥbṭ* the writer is simply focusing on the motif of *gathering* the harvest.[39] Note that the parallel term is *lqt*, which consistently means, 'to gather'.[40] Further, given the image of the vineyard in 27.2-6, it is possible that v. 12 portrays a fruit harvest rather than a grain harvest.[41] Finally, to understand v. 12 as portraying the destruction of the Gentiles is to contradict the eschatological vision of 25.6-10a, which included all peoples.

2. *Restoration and Worship (v. 13)*

The blowing of the *shophar* may be associated with a warning,[42] the epiphany of Yahweh,[43] or as we have here, a call to worship.[44] The writer in Jerusalem anticipates that his brothers and sisters who are lost (*h'bdym*) and banished (*hndḥym*) in exile, will return to Jerusalem to worship Yahweh.[45]

Wildberger disparages the thought of v. 13 as marking a serious decline from the universalistic heights of other parts of the composition.[46] But this is hardly a fair criticism, nor should it surprise us that the attention of this exilic writer is focused on the restoration of his devastated country, and the return of his fellow Jews who had been taken from their homeland. No less an author than Second Isaiah, whose universalistic vision stands at the apogee of OT thought, concludes this composition with the specific mention of the return of his own people (55.12, 13).

D. *The Relationship between 27.2-13 and 24.21–27.1*

Since B. Duhm's seminal analysis of 27.2-13, the common consensus among the scholarly world has been that vv. 2-11 were not a part of the original composition, which properly concludes with vv. 12, 13.[47] This view is based on alleged differences in (1) style, (2) eschatological perspective, and (3) theme.[48]

(1) Style. March argues that none of the mythological motifs from 24.21 occurs in 27.2ff., and that the language is different. He and Rudolph both maintain that the use of proper names in this section is different from the rest of the composition. March is correct that mythological motifs are absent from 27.2ff., but he fails to note that

they are also absent from 26.1-19, which he shows no hesitancy to include in the composition. The presence or absence of certain motifs simply cannot be a criterion for authorship or compositional integrity.

We must express similar doubt about the use of language in this way. For instance, the terminology of vv. 2-5 was chosen, in large part, in order to correspond with the original vineyard song. Similarly, most of the language of vv. 7-11 derives from earlier prophetic traditions. The point is that in the case of vv. 2-11, language is an irrelevant criterion for determining compositional integrity.[49]

The use of the proper names, Jacob and Israel (vv. 6, 9), is not a singular phenomenon. Note the use of 'Mount Zion' and 'Jerusalem' in 24.23 and 'Judah' in 26.1. There are other explanations for the occurrence of the proper names at this point. Perhaps the author was following the pattern established in the first vineyard song which the poet concluded with explicit terms of identification.

Conversely, one can argue that the style of vv. 2-11 is very similar to that of the preceding material. Certainly the obscure manner in which the city of v. 10 is described is reminiscent of the prior three references to the city. Also the employment of older prophetic traditions that we noted in this section is not unlike what we found in the rest of the composition.

(2) Eschatological Perspective. Duhm charged that 'v. 6 belongs neither to the poem (vv. 2-5), nor to the Apocalypse because, next to 25.6-8, it must be considered extremely trivial'.[50] But this is an unfair judgment. To be sure, the imagery in 27.5 is different from that of 25.6-8, but this is not because the perspective is any less universal. Rather it is due to the fact that the author is building on the preceding imagery of the vineyard. We may assume, in the light of the matchless eschatological hope which is developed through the similar imagery of the vine in Isa. 11.1-11, that the thought of 27.6 would not have been regarded by the original readers as trivial.

(3) Theme. The most serious doubts about the integrity of 27.2-11 are due to the different theme which this section conveys. There is no question that the theme of these verses, namely, the reunification of Israel, is quite different from the rest of the composition.[51] But, again, it is doubtful that this is sufficient reason for excluding it. We have only to note that in Ezekiel 37, the portrayal of Judah's salvation and national restoration (vv. 1-14) is followed by an

announcement that the two houses of Israel would be reunited (vv. 15-23). Note Eichrodt's perceptive comment on these verses:

> we should remember that God's saving act would not be complete unless it restored Israel as a whole. The election of that people, once made, must inevitably come to its goal.[52]

May we not assume that our author would similarly follow his announcement of national restoration (26.19; Ezek. 37.1-14) with a statement regarding the reunification of all Israel (27.2-13; Ezek. 37.15-23)? We have already noted this writer's dependence on the prophet Hosea.[53] No doubt he was aware of Hosea's hope for the reuniting of Jacob and Judah, and applied that hope to his own time.[54] Therefore, I conclude that the difference in theme is due to *one* author's comprehensive view of Israel's salvation, rather than to the fragmented thought of two separate writers.

Chapter 5

CONCLUSION

We began this study by noting that Isaiah 24–27 has generally been perceived by the scholarly world as one of the key passages in the origination and development of apocalyptic literature. When one reads almost any Introduction to the Old Testament one consistently finds the assertion that Isa. 24–27 is one of the earliest examples of apocalyptic literature in the OT, if not the earliest. The difficulty with this claim is that it is made consistently *in spite of* the fact that the most basic historical-critical questions have not been resolved.

The proposals for the *date* have ranged from the eighth to the second century. To be sure, most recent scholars have rejected the extreme ends of this continuum and have come to view the sixth–fourth centuries as the most likely provenance. But one would hope for greater precision in the dating of a composition.

The *identity* of the city (or cities) has likewise evaded the interpreter. Samaria, Jerusalem, Carthage, a Moabite city, Babylon, and simply 'city-life' in general have all been proposed, with no consensus having emerged.

The *structure* of these chapters has also proven problematic. Were they simply a loose collection of unrelated parts as B. Duhm had proposed? Subsequent scholars, while accepting much of Duhm's analysis, have detected a greater integrity to this material than had their mentor. And as we noted above, the consensus is such that it is possible now to speak of a compositional unity regarding these four chapters.

Finally, we noted that the question of the *perspective* of the composition has been sharply debated. Scholars have tended to focus *either* on the songs as a reference to a *past* event *or* on the eschatological sayings as an allusion to an undefinable and unhistorical future event.

This study has been an attempt to enter into the scholarly dialogue related to these basic questions. I am now in a position to offer some conclusions.

The composition consists of three major sections. Section A (24.1-20) was written in 587 and was a prediction of the events which devastated Judah. The prophet saw the imminent destruction of Jerusalem as the righteous judgment of Yahweh because of the disobedience of his people (24.5). In drawing upon earlier, Isaianic langugage, this author also perceived these events as the fulfillment of Isaiah's earlier prophecy (24.1-3, 13, verses which bracket the description of the destruction, and which we demonstrated originated with the prophet, Isaiah).

I noted further that there was evidence within the text which suggested that Jerusalem, rather than the whole cosmos, was the focus of Yahweh's attack: language of lament, Mosaic terminology, the phrase, *mśwś h'rṣ* (v. 11) which is an epithet for Jerusalem, the phrase, *bqrb h'rṣ* (v. 13) as an allusion to Jerusalem, and the prophet's reaction of woe in 24.16b. Because Jerusalem was viewed as being the center of the earth, its destruction was perceived as the actual return of chaos. For this reason the prophet drew upon the powerful imagery of the chaos myth in order to communicate the cosmic sense of loss which the historical events of 587 entailed. The destruction of Jerusalem and the ensuing exile could be adequately described only as a return to chaos.

This view marks a major departure from the *communis opinio* which regards this opening section as a prediction of *universal* destruction. It was this universalistic interpretation which catapulted these chapters into the arena of apocalyptic. The evidence for such a view is simply not present in the text.

The *Chaoskampf* is the overriding theme which ties the composition together. With its pattern of threat/battle, victory, and restoration, it lent itself particularly well to the prophet's deep conviction that destruction was not the final word from Yahweh; that the encroachment of chaos was only transitory and would soon give way to the triumph of Yahweh.

It was from this posture of trust and expectation that the prophet composed the second movement (24.21–27.1), which is an announcement of the imminent victory of Yahweh. I have suggested that it was added later during the exile when the writer looked to the future destruction of the city of oppression, Babylon (25.2; 26.5, 6).

He appeals to the old royal theology which was associated with the Jerusalem cult. In the wake of the destruction of Jerusalem, those royal themes were set free from that particular setting, and in the hand of this author of the Isaianic tradition, were employed to portray victorious Yahweh as king over the entire world (25.3-5).

Not only were the royal traditions universalized, they were also eschatologized. Rather than celebrating Yahweh's victory in the past, they are now construed to anticipate a future act of deliverance which the prophet believed would in some measure usher in the new eschatological age (25.6-10a).

Paul Hanson distinguishes between the 'proto-apocalypticism' of Second Isaiah and the 'early-apocalypticism' of Isa. 24–27 (along with Third Isaiah and Zechariah 9 and 10) because, in his view, Second Isaiah held to a 'reasonable optimism' toward the world as 'the context within which the fulfillment of the divine promises would occur', while Isa. 24–27 arose because of the 'loss of this reasonable optimism'. No longer did these people think that 'Yahweh's restoration of his people would occur within the context of this world'.[1]

But our study has demonstrated that the author of Isa. 24–27 was decidedly positive about Yahweh's activity within this world. He believed that the evil city, the historical city of Babylon, would be overthrown (25.1-2; 26.5, 6), that there would be a resurrection of the nation (26.19), and that these historical events would mark the beginning of the new age. G.W. Anderson is correct in reminding us that while the identity of the city in 25.1-2, and 26.5, 6 has proven elusive to most modern interpreters, the original readers 'did not have to stop to make a careful balance of the historical probabilities in an attempt to identify the city: the reference to events and situations within their knowledge must have been evident'.[2] In the aftermath of 587, it would have been evident to any survivor that the hated city was Babylon, and not some supra-historical entity.

Even though critical scholars have often viewed Isa. 24–27 as an early affirmation of the doctrine of individual resurrection, my own analysis has led me to deny this view. In the light of the *communal* nature of the lament (26.7-19), the plea for *national* restoration (26.15), and the use of birth imagery (cf. 26.17, 18) in the rest of the Isaianic corpus as a sign of national rebirth, I have concluded that 26.19 is a reference to national resurrection.

Our investigation of the communal lament in 26.7-19 has revealed no evidence of an inner-community struggle such as O. Plöger and P. Hanson are inclined to imagine in this literature. The people are united in their desire for deliverance from the oppressor. As for the 'inner-community struggle in the period of the Second Temple between visionary and hierocratic elements',[3] it simply is non-existent in this composition.

The author brings his portrayal of the victory of Yahweh to a fitting climax with his direct reference to the myth of the chaos monster in 27.1. Even as Yahweh had defeated the forces of chaos at creation, so again in the great act of recreating his people would the Divine Warrior defeat the chaos monster. Such a metaphorical representation of the hostile political power is reminiscent of Isa. 51.9.

In the third section (27.2-13) the prophet presents the theme of the reunification of Israel as the logical effect of the victory of Yahweh. He believed, as did Jeremiah and Ezekiel (Jer. 31.1-9, 15-20; Ezek. 37.15-23), that the reign of Yahweh would reach its consummation only with the restoration of the nation.

I conclude by stating my view of the relationship between Isa. 24–27 and the phenomenon of apocalyptic in the OT. It is inappropriate to refer to this composition as the 'little apocalypse' or the 'Isaianic apocalypse'. It simply does not exhibit the marks of an apocalypse. If we accept the categories proposed by Hanson, namely, 'proto-apocalyptic' and 'early apocalyptic', along with his criteria for distinguising between the two, then we must deny his view that Isa. 24–27 is 'early-apocalyptic'. It is not pessimistic about history as the realm of Yahweh's activity; it is prior to the Second Temple era; and it does not reflect an inner-community struggle between visionaries and the hierocratic leaders.

Isa. 24–27 belongs to the creative period of the exile, when it became incumbent upon the Jewish community to create new dimensions within their faith which would give meaning to their new situation. The author of this composition drew upon the powerful imagery of the chaos myth in order to communicate the cosmic sense of loss which the historical events of 587 entailed. The destruction of Jerusalem and the ensuing exile were appropriately portrayed as a collapse into chaos. But the chaos myth did more than simply convey the sense of devastation which the community felt; it provided the religious pattern which would give shape to a renewed hope for this exiled community.

APPENDIX

Reconstructed Hebrew Text and Translation

Chapter 24

1. *hnh yhwh bwqq h'rṣ wbwlqh w'wh pnyh whpyṣ yšbyh*
Look! Yahweh is about to devastate the earth
and make it desolate,
and he will twist its surface
and scatter its inhabitants.

2. *whyh k'm kkhn k'bd k'dnyw kšpḥh kgbrth*
kqwnh kmwkr kmlwh klwh knš' k'šr nš' bw
People and priest alike, slave and his master,
maidservant and her mistress, buyer and seller,
lender and borrower, creditor and debtor.

3. *hbwq tbwq h'rṣ whbwz tbwz ky yhwh dbr 't-hdbr hzh*
The earth will be completely devastated
and thoroughly plundered,
for Yahweh has spoken this word.

4. *'blh nblh h'rṣ 'mllh nblh tbl 'mll mrwm h'rṣ*
The earth mourns and withers,
the world languishes and withers;
the high place of the earth languishes.

5. *wh'rṣ ḥnph tḥt yšbyh ky-'brw twrh*
ḥlpw ḥq hprw bryt 'wlm
And the earth lies defiled under its inhabitants,
because they have transgressed the law,
violated the statute, broken the everlasting covenant.

6. *'l-kn 'lh 'klh 'rṣ wy'šmw yšby bh*
'l-kn ḥrw yšby 'rṣ wnš'r 'nwš mz'r
Therefore a curse has devoured the earth,
and its inhabitants have been condemned;
therefore the inhabitants of the earth have dwindled,
and very few are left.

7. *'bl tyrwš 'mllh-gpn n'nḥw kl-śmḥy-lb*
The new wine mourns, the vine languishes,
all the merrymakers groan.

8. *šbt mśwś tpym ḥdl š’wn ’lyzym šbt mśwś knwr*
The joy of tambourines is stilled, the noise of revelers has ceased,
the joy of the lyre is stilled.
9. *bšyr l’ yštw-yyn ymr škr lštyw*
No longer do they drink wine with singing;
the beer has become bitter to those who drink it.
10. *nšbrh qryt-thw sgr kl-byt mbw’*
The city is reduced to chaos,
every house is shut so no one can enter.
11. *ṣwḥh ‘l-hyyn bḥwṣwt ‘rbh kl-śmḥh glh mśwś h’rṣ*
In the streets there is a cry over wine;
all rejoicing has reached its eventide;
the joy of the earth has gone into exile.
12. *nš’r b‘yr šmh wš’yh ykt-š‘r*
Desolation is left in the city,
and the gate is battered into ruins.
13. *ky kh yhyh bqrb h’rṣ btwq h‘mym*
knqp zyt k‘wllt ’m-klh bṣyr
Thus it shall be in the midst of the earth,
among the peoples,
like the beating of an olive tree,
like the gleaning when the grape-harvest is completed.
14. *hmh yś’w qwlm yrnw bg’wn yhwh*
They lift up their voices,
they sing for joy over the majesty of Yahweh,
15. *ṣhlw mym ‘lzw b’rym kbdw yhwh*
b’yy hym šm yhwh ’lhy yśr’l
‘Cry aloud from the west, rejoice in the east,
give glory to Yahweh; in the coastlands of the sea,
to the name of Yahweh, the God of Israel’.
16. *mknp h’rṣ zmrt šm‘nw ṣby lṣdyq*
w’mr rzy-ly rzy-ly ’wy ly bgdym bgdw wbgd bwgdym bgdw
From the ends of the earth we heard songs,
‘Honor to the righteous one’.
But I say, ‘I waste away! I waste away! Woe is me!’
The treacherous deal treacherously,
with treachery the treacherous deal treacherously.
17. *pḥd wpḥt wpḥ ‘lyk ywšb h’rṣ*
Panic and pit and pitfall are upon you,
O inhabitant of the earth.
18. *whyh hns mqwl hpḥd ypl ’l-hpḥt wh‘wlh mtwk hpḥt*
ylkd bpḥ ky-’rbwt mmrwm nptḥw wyr‘šw mwsdy ’rṣ
And it shall be that whoever flees
from the sound of the panic

shall fall into the pit,
and whoever climbs out of the pit
shall be caught in the pitfall.
For the windows from on high have been opened,
and the foundations of the earth are shaken.

19. *r' htr''h 'rṣ pwr htpwrrh 'rṣ mwṭ htmwṭṭh 'rṣ*
Completely broken is the earth,
violently shattered is the earth,
utterly shaken is the earth.

20. *nw' tnw' h'rṣ kškwr whtnwddh kmlwnh*
wkbd 'lyh pš'h wnplh wl'-tsyp qwm
The earth staggers like a drunkard,
it sways like a hut;
and its transgression lies heavy upon it,
it has fallen, and it will not rise again.

21. *whyh bywm hhw' ypqd yhwh 'l-sb' hmrwm bmrwm*
w'l-mlky h'dmh 'l-h'dmh
But it shall be on that day that Yahweh will punish the host of the height in the height,
and the kings of the earth on the earth.

22. *w'spw 'sph 'l-bwr wsgrw 'l-msgr wmrb ymym ypqdw*
And they will be gathered together in the pit,
and they will be locked up in the prison,
and after many days they will be punished.

23. *wḥprh hlbnh wbwsh hḥmh ky-mlk yhwh sb'wt*
bhr ṣywn wbyrwšlm wngd zqnyw kbwd
The moon will be abashed and the sun ashamed,
for Yahweh of hosts will reign on Mount Zion
and in Jerusalem, and before his elders, glory!

Chapter 25

1. *yhwh 'lhy 'th 'rwmmk 'wdh šmk*
ky 'syt pl' 'ṣwt mrḥwq 'mwnh 'mn
Yahweh, you are my God!
I will exalt you, I will praise your name,
for you have done wonderful things,
plans from long ago, faithful and true.

2. *ky śmt 'yr lgl qryh bṣwrh lmplh*
'rmwn zrym m'wr l'wlm l' ybnh
For you have made the city a heap,
the fortified city a ruin,
the palace of aliens a levelled place;

It will never be rebuilt.

3. *'l-kn ykbdwk 'm-'z qwym 'ryṣym yyr'wk*
Therefore, strong peoples will honor you,
ruthless nations will fear you.

4. *ky hyyt m'wz ldl m'wz l'bywn bṣr-lw*
mḥsh mzrm ṣl mḥrb (ky rwḥ 'ryṣym kzrm qr kḥrb bṣywn)
For you have become a refuge to the poor,
a refuge for the needy in his distress,
a shelter from the storm, shade from the heat (for the blast of the ruthless is like a winter storm, like heat in a parched place).

5. *s'wn zrym tkny' (ḥrb bṣl 'b) zmyr 'rysym y'nh*
The uproar of aliens you have subdued,
(as heat in the shade of a cloud),
The victory song of the ruthless is stilled.

6. *w'śh yhwh ṣb'wt lkl-h'mym bhr hzh mšth šmnym*
mšth šmrym šmnym mmḥym šmrym mzqqym
And Yahweh of hosts will prepare for all peoples on this mountain, a feast of rich food, a feast of aged wine; the choicest of rich food, the best of fine wine.

7. *wbl' bhr hzh pny-hlwṭ hlwṭ 'l-kl-h'mym*
whmskh hnswkh 'l-kl-hgwym
And he will destroy on this mountain the veil
that is drawn over all the peoples.
The covering which is spread over all the nations.

8. *wbl' hmwt lnṣḥ wmḥh 'dny yhwh dm'h m'l kl-pnym*
wḥrpt 'mw ysyr m'l kl-h'rṣ ky yhwh dbr
And he will swallow up death forever,
And the Lord Yahweh will wipe away the tears
from every face, and the reproach of his people
he will remove from all the earth,
for Yahweh has spoken.

9. *w'mr bywm hhw' hnh 'lhynw zh qwynw lw wywšy'nw zh yhwh qwynw lw ngylh wnśmḥh byšw'tw*
And they will say on that day,
'See! This is our God; we waited for him
and he has delivered us.
This is Yahweh; we waited for him;
Let us rejoice and be glad in his deliverance'.

10. *ky-tnwḥ yd yhwh bhr hzh*
(wndwš mw'b tḥtyw khdwš mtbn bmw mdmnh [11.] *wprś ydyw bqrbw k'šr yprś hśḥh lśḥwt whšpyl g'wtw 'm 'rbwt ydyw* [12.] *wmbṣr mśgb ḥwmtyk hšḥ hšpyl hgy' l'rṣ 'd 'pr*
For the hand of Yahweh will rest on this mountain, (But Moab will be trodden down in its place, like the trampling of straw in a dung

pit. [11.] And he will spread out his hands in the midst of it as a swimmer spreads his hands to swim; and he [God] will humble his pride together with his insidious ways. [12.] And the high fortifications of your walls he will bring down, he will bring it low, cast it to the ground, even to the dust).

Chapter 26

1. *bywm hhw' ywšr hšyr-hzh b'rṣ yhwdh*
'yr 'z-lnw yšw'h ywšt hwmwt wḥl
In that day this song will be sung
in the land of Judah:
We have a strong city,
Victory is established
Walls and rampart (in place);
2. *ptḥw s'rym wyb' gwy-ṣdyq šmr 'mnym*
Open the gates, let the righteous nation enter,
the one which keeps faith;
3. *yṣrw smwk tṣr šlwm šlwm ky bk bṭwḥ*
Its character is steadfast,
you will keep (it) in peace,
peace because it trusts in you.
4. *bṭḥw byhwh 'dy-'d byh ky yhwh ṣwr 'wlmym*
Trust in Yahweh forever,
in Yah, for Yahweh is an everlasting rock.
5. *ky hšḥ yšby mrwm qryh nśgbh yšpylnh*
yšpylh 'd-'rs ygy'nh 'd-'pr
Indeed, he has brought low
the inhabitants of the height,
the lofty city he casts down;
he casts it down to the ground,
he throws it down to the dust.
6. *trmsnh rgl rgly 'ny p'my dlym*
Feet trample it, the feet of the poor,
the steps of the needy.
7. *'rh lṣdyq myšrym m'gl yšr tpls*
The way for the righteous is level,
the path of the upright you make smooth.
8. *'p 'rḥ mšpṭyk yhwh qwynw*
lšmk wlzkrk t'wt-npšnw
Yes, O Yahweh, we wait for the way of your judgments,
your name and your memory are the desire of our soul.
9. *npšy 'wytyk blylh 'p-rwḥy bqrby 'šḥrk*
ky k'šr mšpṭyk l'rṣ ṣdq lmdw yšby tbl

My soul longs for you in the night,
my spirit within me seeks you at dawn.
For when your judgments correct the earth,
the inhabitants of the world learn righteousness.

10. *yḥn rš' bl-lmd ṣdq b'rṣ nkḥwt y'wl wbl-yr'h g'wt yhwh*
If the wicked is shown favor
he will not learn justice,
he will pervert rightness on the earth,
and he will not see the majesty of Yahweh.

11. *yhwh rmh ydk bl-yḥzywn yhzw*
wybšw qn't-'m 'p-'š ṣryk t'klm
Yahweh, your hand is raised,
they do not see (it), but let them see,
and let the antagonists of (your) people be abashed.
Yes, may fire for your enemies consume them.

12. *yhwh tšpt šlwm lnw ky gm kl-m'śynw p'lt lnw*
Yahweh, may you establish peace for us,
since you have also requited all our misdeeds.

13. *yhwh 'lhynw b'lwnw 'dnym zwltk lbd-bk nzkyr šmk*
Yahweh, our God,
other masters besides you have been ruling us,
but we acknowledge your name alone.

14. *mtym bl-yḥyw rp'ym bl-yqmw*
lkn pqdt wtšmydm wt'bd kl-zkr lmw
The dead do not live, the shades do not arise,
therefore, may you attack and destroy them,
may you wipe out all remembrance of them.

15. *yspt lgwy yhwh yspt lgwy nkbdt rḥqt kl-qṣwy-'rṣ*
May you increase the nation,
may you increase the nation,
may you be glorified,
may you extend all the borders of the land.

16. *yhwh bṣr pqdnwk ṣ'qnw lhṣ mwsrk lnw*
Yahweh, in distress we sought you,
we cried out in anguish at your chastisement of us.

17. *kmw hrh tqryb lldt tḥyl tz'q bḥblyh kn hyynw mpnyk yhwh*
Like a woman with child, when she is near her time,
who writhes and cries out in her pain,
so have we become because of you, O Yahweh.

18. *hrynw ḥlnw kmw yldnw rwḥ yšw't bl-n'śh 'rṣ*
wbl-yplw yšby tbl
We were with child, we writhed, we brought forth wind;
We have brought no deliverance to the land,
and no inhabitants of the world have been born.

19. *yḥyw mtyk nblty tqwmwn hqyṣw wrnnw śkny ʿpr*
ky ṭl ʾwrt ṭlk wʾrṣ rpʾym tpyl
Your dead shall live, my body shall rise.
Awake and sing for joy, O dwellers in the dust,
for your dew is a dew of light,
and earth will give birth to the shades.
20. *lk ʿmy bʾ bḥdryk wsgr dltyk bʿdk*
ḥby kmʿt-rgʿ ʿd-yʿbwr-zʿm
Go, my people, enter your chambers,
and shut your doors behind you.
Hide for a little while, until the wrath is past.
21. *ky-hnh yhwh yṣʾ mmqwmw lpqd ʿwn yšb-hʾrṣ ʿlyw*
wglth hʾrṣ ʾt-dmyh wlʾ-hrwgyh
For Yahweh is about to come forth from his
place to punish the inhabitants of the earth
for their iniquity,
and the earth will disclose its bloodshed,
and will no longer cover its slain.

Chapter 27

1. *bywm hhwʾ ypqd yhwh bḥrbw hqšh whgdwlh whḥzqh*
ʿl lwytn nḥš brḥ wʿl lwytn nḥš ʿqltwn
whrg ʾt-htnyn ʾšr bym
In that day Yahweh with his sharp and great and strong sword will punish Leviathan, the fleeing serpent, Leviathan, the twisting serpent, and he will slay the dragon which is in the sea.
2. *bywm hhwʾ krm ḥmd ʿnw-lh*
And there shall be in that day,
a delightful vineyard, sing of it.
3. *ʾny yhwh nṣrh lrgʿym ʾšqnh*
pn ypqd rʿ ʿlyh lylh wywm ʾṣrnh
I, Yahweh am its keeper, regularly I water it.
Lest evil be visited upon it,
I watch it night and day.
4. *ḥmh ʾyn ly my-ytnny šmyr wšyt*
bmlḥmh ʾpšʿh bh ʾṣytnh yḥd
I have no wrath.
If I were given thorns and briars,
I would march against them in battle;
I would burn them up together.
5. *ʾw yḥzq bmʿwzy yʿśh šlwm ly šlwm yʿśh-ly*
Or let that one grasp my protection,
let him make peace with me,

peace, let him make with me.

6. *hb'ym yšrš y'qb yṣyṣ wprḥ yśr'l*
wml'w pny-tbl tnwbh
In the coming (days),
Jacob will take root, Israel will blossom and bud,
and they will fill the whole world with fruit.

7. *hkmkt mkhw hkhw 'm-khrg hrgyw hrg*
Was he beaten as the one who beat him was beaten?
Or was he slain, as his slayers were slain?

8. *bs's'h bšlḥh yrybnh hgh brwḥw hqšh bywm qdym*
When he drove her away, cast her forth,
he contended with her;
he removed her with his fierce blast
on the day of the east wind.

9. *lkn bz't ykpr 'wn-y'qb wzh kl kprw hsr ḥṭ'tw*
bśwmw kl-'bny mzbḥ k'bny-gr mnpṣwt l'-yqmw 'šrym wḥmnym
Therefore by this will the iniquity of Jacob be covered,
and this will be his full ransom to remove his sin:
when he makes all the altar stones
like pulverized chalk stones,
so no asherim or incense altars remain standing.

10. *ky 'yr bṣwrh bdd nwh mšlḥ wn'zb kmdbr*
šm yr'h 'gl wšm yrbṣ wklh s'pyh
For the fortified city is solitary,
a habitation, deserted and forsaken like the desert;
there the calf grazes,
and there it lies down and feeds on its branches.

11. *bybš qṣyrh tšbrnh nšym b'wt m'yrwt 'wth*
ky l' 'm-bynwt hw'
'l-kn l'-yrḥmnw 'šhw wyṣrw l' yḥnnw
When its limbs dry up, women break them
when they come to make a fire with them.
For this is a people without understanding;
therefore their maker will have no compassion on them,
and their creator will show them no favor.

12. *whyh bywm hhw'*
yḥbṭ yhwh mšblt hnhr 'd-nhl mṣrym
w'tm tlqṭw l'ḥd 'ḥd bny yśr'l
And it shall be in that day, that Yahweh will thresh
from the flowing river to wadi of Egypt,
and you shall be gathered one by one, children of Israel.

13. *whyh bywm hhw' ytq' bšwpr gdwl*
wb'w h'bdym b'rṣ 'šwr whndḥym b'rṣ mṣrym
whštḥww lyhwh bhr hqdš byrwšlm

And it shall be in that day,
when the great horn is blown, they will come:
those who were lost in the land of Assyria,
and those who were banished to the land of Egypt,
and they will worship Yahweh on the holy mountain, in Jerusalem.

NOTES

Notes to Chapter 1

1. In the area of NT theology, note E. Käsemann's well-known assertion that, 'Apocalyptic was the mother of all Christian theology', in his essay, 'The Beginnings of Christan Theology', *New Testament Questions of Today* (Philadelphia: Fortress Press, 1969), p. 102. See also his essay, 'On the Subject of Primitive Christian Apocalyptic', in the same volume (pp. 108-37). Cf. also the major contribution in this area by J.C. Beker, *Paul the Apostle, The Triumph of God in Life and Thought* (Philadelphia: Fortress Press, 1980). In the area of OT studies, see the widely acclaimed work by P. Hanson, *The Dawn of Apocalyptic* (Philadelphia: Fortress Press, 1979).

2. This view has been developed in a comprehensive way by Hanson (*Dawn*), and is a proper corrective to D.S. Russell who attributed far too much influence to Iranian religious thought in *The Method and Message of Jewish Apocalyptic* (Philadelphia: Westminster Press, 1964) (see especially p. 18 and the term, 'Persia' in the subject index).

3. This is the view of W.R. Millar, *Isaiah 24–27 and the Origin of Apocalyptic* (Missoula, Montana: Scholars Press, 1976). He is dependent on his teacher, F.M. Cross, who in an addendum to his highly significant book, *Canaanite Myth and Hebrew Epic* (Cambridge, MA: Harvard University Press, 1975), entitled 'A Note on the Study of Apocalyptic Origins', writes, 'In Second Isaiah, Isaiah 24–27 and 34–35, all from the sixth-century . . . we discern a vast transformation in the character of prophecy' (p. 345). Later he concludes, 'I think it is accurate to say that it is in this late Exilic and early post-Exilic literature that we detect the rudimentary traits and motives of apocalypticism' (p. 346). Cf. also P. Hanson, *Dawn*, p. 313, and the earlier, seminal work by O. Plöger, *Theocracy and Eschatology* (Richmond, VA: John Knox Press, 1968, trans S. Rudman, from the second German edition, 1962 [first edn, 1959]). Plöger traces the development of Apocalyptic from Isa. 24–27 through 'Trito-Zechariah' (Zech. 12–14), Joel, and the book of Daniel. That Isa. 24–27 plays a pivotal role in the emergence of OT apocalyptic is asserted by most Introductions to the OT.

4. Because the determination of the date of the composition has depended so largely on the identity given to the city, I shall discuss these two topics together.

5. Several of the reasons for this conclusion were stated by W. Rudolph, *Jesaja 24–27* (BWANT 9; Stuttgart: W. Kohlhammer Verlag, 1933), pp. 60-61. While I would not subscribe to every point, I accept his overall argument as sound. The very capable conservative scholar, F. Delitzsch, was

convinced by the force of such arguments, and attributed these chapters to 'a disciple of Isaiah who in this case surpasses his master', *The Prophecies of Isaiah* (Edinburgh: T&T Clark, 1894), p. 419. More recently, E.J. Young continues to affirm the Isaianic authorship of these chapters, though he maintains that at least portions of chs. 24–27 deal with the exile of 587, *The Book of Isaiah* (NIV 2; Grand Rapids: Eerdmans, 1964), pp. 243, 244. The Roman Catholic scholar, E.J. Kissane, has argued that Isa. 24–27 reflects the conflict between Israel and Assyria in the eighth century, *The Book of Isaiah* I (Dublin: Richview Press, 1941); but few interpreters have been convinced.

6. Cf. F.M. Cross, *Canaanite Myth*, pp. 326-30.

7. B. Duhm, *Das Buch Jesaia* (Göttingen: Vandenhoeck & Ruprecht, 1892), p. 172; he proposed the period between 113-105 BCE, and the destruction of Samaria by John Hyrcanus; D.O. Procksch, *Jesaia* (KAT 9/1; Leipzig: D.W. Scholl Verlag, 1930), p. 345; he suggested the fall of Carthage in 146, and based this identification primarily on the reference in 24.14, 'from the west'.

8. O. Eissfeldt, *The Old Testament: An Introduction* (New York: Harper and Row, 1965), p. 326. E.S. Mulder was more precise, identifying the city as Moabite Dibon, overthrown by the Nabateans in 270, *Die Teologie van die Jesaja-Apokalypse, Jesaja 24–27* (Groningen, Djakarta: J.B. Wolters, 1954), pp. 91-93.

9. W. Kessler, *Gott geht es um das Ganze, Jesaja 56–66 und Jesaja 24–27* (BAT 19; Stuttgart: Calwer Verlag, 1960), pp. 150, 169.

10. O. Plöger, *Theocracy and Eschatology*, p. 56.

11. *Ibid.*, p. 69

12. *Ibid.*, pp. 75-78.

13. Cf. my discussion in the Excursus in ch. 3.

14. W. Rudolph, *Jes. 24–27*, pp. 61-64.

15. O. Kaiser, *Isaiah 13–39* (OTL; Philadelphia: Westminster Press, 1974), pp. 177, 181.

16. *Ibid.* Cf. p. 181 on 24.10, p. 197 on 25.1-5 and p. 206 on 26.1-6. He dismisses 27.10 as 'completely obscure' (p. 177).

17. *Ibid.*, p. 179

18. J. Lindblom, *Die Jesaja-Apokalypse, Jes. 24–27* (Lund: Gleerup, 1938), pp. 72-84.

19. H. Wildberger, *Jesaja* (BKAT 10/2; 10 Neukirchen-Vluyn: Neukirchener Verlag, 1978), p. 957.

20. *Ibid.*, p. 911

21. W.E. March, 'A Study of Two Prophetic Compositions in Is. 24.1–27.1' (Unpublished Dissertation, Union Theological Seminary, N.Y., 1966), pp. 199-221.

22. *Ibid.*, pp. 37-42.

23. *Ibid.*, p. 93

24. *Ibid.*, pp. 173-93.

25. F.M. Cross, *Canannite Myth*, p. 345; P. Hanson, *Dawn*, p. 313. The most extensive application of this method to Isa. 24–27 has been carried out by W.R. Millar, *Origin of Apocalyptic*. In my view, the claims for pinpoint accuracy in dating passages to a precise decade on the basis of this analysis, such as is found in Hanson's *Dawn*, are highly questionable. Nevertheless, the more general claims for a particular period have a high degree of validity.

26. P. Hanson (*Dawn*, p. 314) proposes Jerusalem but states that 'this hypothesis requires closer examination'. Cf. W.R. Millar, *Origin of Apocalyptic*, pp. 115-19. Both authors are dependent on the theory espoused by Plöger, namely, that there is a division within the Jewish community between the 'visionaries' and the 'oppressive leaders'. To the visionaries, who were responsible for Isa. 24–27, 'the Jerusalem of reality and the Zion of faith . . . remained far apart' (Millar, p. 119). But this theory, while applicable to later documents, cannot be sustained in regard to Isa. 24–27, as we will demonstrate in ch. 3.

27. Cf. J. Neusner, 'Judaism in a Time of Crisis, Four Responses to the Destruction of the Second Temple', *Judaism* 21 (1972), pp. 313-27.

28. In addition to the authors cited above who support this view, cf. also G.W. Anderson, 'Isaiah XXIV–XXVII Reconsidered', *VTS* 9 (1963), p. 126; H. Ringgren, 'Some Observations on Style and Structure in the Isaiah Apocalypse', *ASTI* 9 (1973), p. 114; B. Otzen, 'Traditions and Structures of Isaiah XXIV–XXVII', *VT* 24 (1974), p. 206.

29. B. Duhm, *Jesaia*, p. 172.

30. G. Hylmö, *De s.k. profetiska liturgiernas rytm, stil och komposition*. His work was not available to me, but cf. the critique by W. Rudolph, *Jes. 24–27*, pp. 35, 36 or J. Lindblom, *Jes.-Apok.*, pp. 67-69.

31. J. Lindblom, *Jes.-Apok.*, p. 68

32. *Ibid.*, p. 69.

33. G. Fohrer, 'Der Aufbau der Apokalypse des Jesajabuchs, Jes. 24–27', *CBQ* 25 (1963), pp. 34-45; W.E. March, *Two Prophetic Compositions*.

34. We have already noted Hylmö's failure to do justice to all of the material. March is forced to consider 27.2-13 extraneous to the composition, and most interpreters would deny his and Fohrer's assertion that 24.1-20 is a prophetic liturgy.

35. O. Kaiser, *Isaiah*, pp. 177, 178; H. Wildberger, *Jesaja*, p. 893.

36. H. Wildberger, *Jesaja*, pp. 896ff.

37. *Ibid.*, p. 904.

38. In addition to Kaiser and Wildberger, those who engage in this speculative enterprise are M.-L. Henry, *Glaubenskrise und Glaubensbewahrung in den Dichtungen der Jesaja-apokalypse* (BWANT 86; Stuttgart: W. Kohlhammer, 1967); O. Plöger, *Theocracy and Eschatology*; J. Vermeylen, *La composition littéraire de l'apocalypse d'Isaïe (Is., XXIX–XXVII)*, ALBO Serv. V, Fasc. 14 (1974).

39. Note G.W. Anderson's prudent defense of the 'substantial unity' of these chapters, which he describes as 'the unity of a prophetic response to a particular situation', in 'Isaiah XXIV–XXVII Reconsidered', p. 122.

40. J. Lindblom, *Jes.-Apok.*, pp. 42, 53, 26.

41. W. Rudolph, *Jes. 24–27*, pp. 34, 35.

42. O. Plöger, *Theocracy and Eschatology*, pp. 69, 70.

43. O. Kaiser, *Isaiah*, p. 177; H. Wildberger, *Jesaja*, pp. 957, 977.

44. In my view, the perfect tenses in 27.7, 8 indicate that 27.10 does not fit this futuristic pattern, but is a reference to a past event.

45. Cf. Jer. 31.1-9, 15-20; Ezek. 37.15-23.

Notes to Chapter 2

1. Those who extend the first major unit through v. 13 are G.B. Gray, *Isaiah*, pp. 408-14; E.J. Kissane, *Isaiah*, p. 281; O. Plöger, *Theocracy and Eschatology*, pp. 56, 57; O. Kaiser, *Isaiah*, p. 181; H. Wildberger, *Jesaja*, pp. 9, 12ff.

2. W.E. March, *Two Prophetic Compositions*, p. 20.

3. *Ibid.*

4. *Ibid.*, pp. 26, 27.

5. G.B. Gray, *Isaiah*, pp. 417-19.

6. W.R. Millar, *Origin of Apoc.*, p. 31.

7. W.E. March, *Two Prophetic Compositions*, pp. 39-40.

8. This is supported by O. Kaiser (*Isaiah*, p. 181), and also by O. Plöger (*Theocracy and Eschatology*, p. 57), who notes that all of the verses in this unit 'have been made an integral part of the narrative by the author of our chapter. Thus, the section 24.8-12, together with the bridge verses, 7 and 13, is to be interpreted as a continuation of 24.1-6'. H. Wildberger has also noted the compositional nature of Isa. 24–27, though he insists that it underwent an extensive 'Wachstumsprozess', or growth process (pp. 893, 896; cf. my Introduction).

9. J. Lindblom, *Jes.-Apok.*, p. 13; W. Rudolph, *Jes. 24–27*, p. 30, though he recognizes a break after v. 3 as indicated by the fact that he designates vv. 4f. as the second strophe; M.-L. Henry, *Glaubenskrise*, pp. 116ff.

10. H. Wildberger, *Jesaja*, p. 897.

11. O. Plöger notes the difficulty: 'there is a striking affirmation in 24.3 that Yahweh has spoken, although no word of Yahweh has been recorded either preceding (as in Isa. 1.20) or following (as in Isa. 1.12)' (*Theocracy and Eschatology*, p. 55).

12. P.L. Redditt's terminology (*Isa. 24–27*, p. 73).

13. G.N.M. Habets (*Die grosse Jes.-Apok.*, p. 56) has argued that v. 7 is a transitional phrase joining vv. 1-6 and 8-12. This may be true though it seems to be an artificial arrangement.

14. B. Duhm, *Jesaia*, p. 175.

15. This is the view of W.E. March, *Two Prophetic Compositions*, p. 20; P.L. Redditt, *Isa. 24–27*, pp. 68-70; G. Fohrer, *Das Buch Jesaja* (Zürich: Zwingli Verlag, 1962) p. 3, calls it an 'eschatological judgment'.

16. H. Wildberger (*Jesaja*, p. 904) 'das Weltgericht'; J. Lindblom (*Jes.-Apok.*, p. 13), 'Eschatologisches Gedicht', 'Weltkatastrophe'; W. Rudolph (*Jes. 24–27*, p. 27) 'Weltgericht'.

17. P.L. Redditt, *Isa. 24–27*, p. 75.

18. Cf. n. 16 above.

19. Cf. the article by J.J.M. Roberts, 'Form, Syntax, and Redaction in Isaiah 1.2-20', *PSB* 3 (1982), pp. 293-306.

20. D.R. Hillers, *Treaty-Curses and the Old Testament Prophets* (BO 16; Rome: Pontifical Biblical Institute, 1964), p. 89.

21. *Ibid.*, p. 57.

22. *Ibid.*, p. 62.

23. *Ibid.*, p. 71.

24. P. Lohmann, 'Die selbständigen lyrischen Abschnitte in Jes. 24–27', *ZAW* (1917), pp. 22-27.

25. *Ibid.*, p. 25.

26. J. Lindblom, *Jes.-Apok.*, p. 19.

27. *Ibid.*

28. *Ibid.*

29. Cf. O. Eissfeldt, *Introduction*, pp. 95, 96, for examples of comparison.

30. O. Plöger, *Theocracy and Eschatology*, p. 56.

31. C. Westermann, *Praise and Lament in the Psalms* (Atlanta: John Knox Press, 1981), pp. 173-75.

32. See also above (p. 20) where I note that his formal designation requires a rather strained understanding of vv. 14-16a.

33. O. Eissfeldt, *Introduction*, pp. 95, 96.

34. *Ibid.*, p. 95.

35. W. Holladay, *Isaiah: Scroll of a Prophetic Heritage* (Grand Rapids: Eerdmans, 1978), p. 195.

36. *Ibid.*

37 H. Wildberger, *Jesaja*, p. 917. Wildberger correctly insists that this phenomenon shows the dependence of Isa. 24–27 on the earlier Isaianic tradition, rather than being support for Isaianic authenticity.

38. S. Hurvitz, *A Linguistic Study of the Relationship between the Priestly Source and the Book of Ezekiel, A New Approach to an Old Problem* (Paris: J. Gabalda, 1982) and R. Polzin, *Late Biblical Hebrew, Toward an Historical Typology of Biblical Hebrew Prose* (Missoula, Montana: Scholars Press, 1976). Both authors make a distinction between lexical and stylistic features: the former may be imitated quite easily, while the latter may not.

39. G.B. Gray, *Isaiah*, p. 408. It should be noted that Gray goes on to reject this view, suggesting that the author was using figurative imagery.

40. R.E. Clements, 'The Prophecies of Isaiah and the Fall of Jerusalem in

587 BC', *VT* 30 (1980), pp. 421-36. His thesis is that the events of 587 were 'pivotal' in the final shaping of the book of Isaiah.

41. Cf. the Introduction. These scholars would include Rudolph, Lindblom, Wildberger, Henry, Gray and others.

42. W. Gesenius, *Jesaia*, pp. 761ff.; R. Lowth, *Isaiah*, pp. 42-43, 263; R. Smend, 'Anmerkungen zu Jes. 24–27', pp. 163ff.; R.B.Y. Scott, *Isaiah*, p. 298. It should be noted that in the pre-critical era there were several commentators who held to this view, as indicated by the fact that J. Calvin refers to those who 'view this as referring to Israel' (*Commentary*, p. 165).

43. W. Gesenius, *Jesaia*, p. 763.

44. R. Lowth, *Isaiah*, p. 263

45. R. Smend, 'Anmerkungen zu Jes. 24–27', p. 166.

46. R.B.Y. Scott, *Isaiah*, p. 298.

47. This conclusion is supported by O. Kaiser, who notes 'the remarkable intermingling of the prophecy of judgment of the world and of the imminent conquest and destruction of Babylon' (*Isaiah*, p. 9).

48. Cf. also R. Smend, 'Anmerkungen', p. 166 n. 3, 'Ich behaupte übrigens nur, daß *tbl* nicht notwendig die ganze Erde umfaßt'.

49. E.J. Kissane (*Isaiah*, p. 279), refers to 'Modern critics who take 1ff. literally as a description of judgment on all nations'. He later suggests that 'the prophet is really speaking of the world-judgment as it affects Israel' (p. 280). Earlier, he entitled the opening section: 'The Ruin of Judah' (p. 271). Cf. W.E. March, *Two Prophetic Compositions*, pp. 27-29.

50. Cf. Isa. 5.25; 13.1-16, now applied to the people of Babylon; 14.26; 18.3; 34.4, 5; Jer. 4.23-28; Amos 9.5-10; Mic. 1.2-7; Zeph. 1.1-6.

51. Cf. W.E. March, *Two Prophetic Compositions*, p. 31, who holds a similar view to my own; he refers to the 'accompanying terminology'. Most commentators recognize the 'Mosaic flavor' of these terms (though they treat them differently than I do), and it is unnecessary to list them all here.

52. Cf. Neh. 9.13; Exod. 16.28; 18.16, 20; Lev. 26.46; Ezek. 43.11; 44.5, 24; Ps. 105.45. The listing of these occurrences of the plural form is in some measure a concession to the majority view that the plural form was in the original text but LXX and Syriac read the singular, *twrk*.

53. Cf. Mandelkern's *Concordance*.

54. J. Schmidt advances a similar argument, especially regarding point 3, *Der Ewigkeitsbegriff im Alten Testament* (AA 13; Münster, 1940), pp. 69-70.

55. It is often assumed that the covenant mentioned here refers to a covenant which Sennacherib (or according to Kaiser [*Isaiah*, pp. 342-45] a tyrant in the Hellenistic period!) made with Israel, but later broke. But Kissane (*Isaiah*, p. 375) has argued convincingly that the covenant refers to the covenant between Judah and Yahweh.

56. G. von Rad, *Genesis* (OTL; Philadelphia: Westminster Press, 1972), pp. 133, 134.

57. G. von Rad, *Old Testament Theology*, II (New York: Harper and Row, 1965), p. 347. In a related discussion he refers to such passages as Jer. 25.15ff.; 46-51; Joel 4.1ff. (3.1ff., Eng.); Hag. 2.21, but these are judgments against the nations, not a judgment that would revert the world order to a state of chaos, and thus bring to an end the present age.

58. I concur with E.J. Kissane, who insists that 'the law against bloodshed is quite independent of the covenant' (*Isaiah*, p. 279).

59. Cf. the Introduction.

60. R.E. Clements, *Isaiah 1-39* (The New Century Bible Commentary; Grand Rapids: Eerdmans, 1980), p. 202. It is important to note that the intended translation is not 'city of chaos' as it is commonly rendered. Rather, there is good reason for regarding *thw* as part of the predicate. LXX reads *hērēmōthē pasa polis*, 'enemy city is made desolate'. The Peshitta has 'the city is plundered'. And the Targum has *'ytbrh qrthwn ṣdy't*, 'their city is broken down, it is desolate'. *thw* is consistently regarded as part of the predicate and not as part of the subject. *thw* does not refer to the character of the city, but to the fate which the city will experience when the advancing armies execute Yahweh's judgment.

61. H. Wildberger concurs with this view. He writes, 'Die Analyse hat ergeben, daß die Stadt von 10ff. kaum dieselbe sein dürfte wie die feindliche Stadt in 25.1ff and 26.1ff' (*Jesaja*, p. 926). B. Duhm concludes that Jerusalem is the city alluded to in 24.10, in part, for the following reason: 'Denn wenn eine andere Stadt gemeint wäre, so müsste sie auf irgend eine Weise näher bezeichnet sein, wie es z.B. 25.2, 4 geschieht' (*Jesaia*, pp. 174, 175). For an opposing view, see E.S. Mulder, *Die Teologie van die Jesaja-Apokalipse, Jesaja 24–27* (Groningen: J.B. Walters, 1954), pp. 64-65, 78ff.

62. O. Plöger, *Theocracy and Eschatology*, p. 56. He is supported by G. Fohrer, *Jesaja*, p. 8, and his article, 'Der Aufbau der Apokalypse des Jesajabuchs, Jes. 24–27', *CBQ* 25 (1963), p. 41. Cf. also R. Hahnhart, 'Die jahwefeindliche Stadt', *Festschrift für W. Zimmerli* (BZAT; ed. H. Donner, R. Hahnhart, and R. Smend; Göttingen: Vandenhoeck & Ruprecht, 1977), p. 152; he refers to the destruction of the city 'als Typos der Zerstörung menschlicher Gemeinschaft'.

63. H. Wildberger, *Jesaja*, p. 930. Cf. G.N.M. Habets, *Die grosse Jes.-Apok.*, pp. 63, 64; he appeals to the reading of the LXX, *pasa polis*, as support for his view that no specific city was intended. But in light of the tendency toward 'free translation' on the part of LXX, more support is required.

64. Only rarely in the non-prophetic literature does this term simply mean 'depart' (Prov. 27.25; Job 20.28). Indeed, the very fact aht the phrase is infelicitous suggests that a particular nuance was intended: in this case an allusion to the exile.

65. The only other occurrence of *glh* is Isa. 20.4.

66. See below, Chapter 4.

67. W. Rudolph, *Jes. 24–27*, p. 11, 'gefangengeführt ist die Wonne der Erde = Jerusalem (Ps. 48.3), eine Glosse, die unter der Stadt fälschlich Jerusalem verstand und die Erwähnung des Exils vermisste'. W.E. March also mentions this point (*Two Prophetic Compositions*, p. 44).

68. H. Wildberger, *Jesaja*, p. 926.

69. W. Elder ('A Theological-Historical Study of Is. 24–27' [Unpublished Dissertation, Baylor University, 1974], pp. 111-20) has argued extensively that the language in 24.7-12 is cultic, and more specifically, is reflective of the royal cult of Jerusalem. Some of his observations are, in my judgment, quite dubious. For example, he holds that *bḥwṣwt*, in the context of wine and celebration, implies the imagery of the 'festal streets of Jerusalem on which the cultic procession regularly traveled' (p. 113). Further, he suggests that *š'r* is a 'cultic metonym'. It is possible that the cultic allusions to Jerusalem's cult are in the text, but in light of the fact that wine, streets, gates, etc. are universally a part of city-life, it is impossible to base the identity of Jerusalem on these observations.

70. J. Lindblom, *Jes.-Apok.*, pp. 20, 21; also B. Otzen, 'Traditions and Structures of Isaiah 24–27', *VT* 24 (1974), p. 202; Of course, the seminal work in this area is that of H. Gressmann, *Der Ursprung der israelitisch-jüdischen Eschatologie* (Göttingen: Vandenhoeck & Ruprecht, 1905), see especially pp. 183ff. Cf. also W.E. March, *Two Prophetic Compositions*, p. 45; W. Kessler (*Gott geht es um das Ganze*, p. 134) conveys the view of many interpreters: 'Die Ausdrücke "in der Mitte der Erde", "Mitten unter den Völkern" beziehen sich offenbar auf Juda und Jerusalem. Hier, wo der wahre, lebendige Gott verehrt wird, ist der "Nabel der Erde", ihr eigentlicher Mittelpunkt'.

71. J. Lindblom, *Jes.-Apok.*, p. 21.

72. P.L. Redditt, *Isa. 24–27*, in a footnote, p. 87.

73. 'Center' rather than 'navel' is the more appropriate term. The Hebrew word for navel is *tbwr*.

74. H. Wildberger, *Jesaja*, p. 929.

75. I recognize that arguments based on lexical studies are somewhat tenuous. Nevertheless, the evidence which I cite, while it can not confirm my point, does lend support to the overall argument.

76. Cf. Jer. 4.28, 12.4, 11; 14.2; 23.10; Hos. 4.3; 10.5; Amos 1.2; 5.16, 17; 8.8; Lam. 1.4; 2.8; 3.15.

77. *nbl* occurs in the Qal eleven times in the prophetic literature. Nine of these are in the Isaianic corpus. Of these, the two occurrences found in 24.4; 40.7, 8 are general references, and 64.5 refers to Zion. Jer. 8.13 refers to the doom of Judah, and Ezek. 47.12 to the restoration of Judah. Isa. 34.4 deviates from the pattern by referring to the host of heaven.

78. Cf. Exod. 2.23; Ezek. 9.4; 21.11, 12 (21.6, 7, Eng.).

79. Cf. A. Weiser, *The Psalms, A Commentary* (OTL; Philadelphia: Westminster Press, 1962), pp. 487, 488.

80. Note also Isa. 32.15; 57.15; Jer. 17.12; 25.30; Mic. 6.6; Pss. 7.8; 92.9; 93.4; 144.7; Lam. 1.13.

81. I mention this here only briefly, allowing for fuller treatment when this pericope is considered later.

82. Cf. the excellent discussion and summary of views in G.N.M. Habets, *Die grosse Jes.-Apok.*, pp. 69-74.

83. G.B. Gray, *Isaiah*, p. 415.

84. W. Rudolph, *Jes. 24-27*, p. 31.

85. G.B. Gray, *Isaiah*, p. 416.

86. *Ibid.*, p. 415. We must recognize that vv. 14-16a may have been an originally independent unit that was inserted here for no apparent reason, which would explain why this section has been so problematic for interpreters. As tempting as this 'solution' to a very thorny problem might be, we, along with most interpreters, cannot subscribe to it.

87. W. Rudolph, *Jes. 24-27*, p. 31; O. Procksch, *Jesaia*, p. 311; H. Wildberger, *Jesaja*, p. 934.

88. J. Lindblom, *Jes.-Apok.*, p. 21; supported by W. Kessler, *Gott geht es um das Ganze*, p. 134.

89. *Ibid.*, p. 23.

90. B. Duhm, *Jesaia*, p. 176; cf. G.B. Gray, *Isaiah*, p. 418 for the quotation of Marti.

91. Cf. O. Plöger, for a similar criticism, *Theocracy and Eschatology*, p. 57.

92. W.R. Millar, *Origin of Apocalyptic*, p. 112.

93. H. Wildberger, *Jesaja*, p. 933.

94. *Ibid.*, p. 940.

95. O. Plöger, *Theocracy and Eschatology*, p. 58.

96. G.B. Gray, *Isaiah*, p. 363.

97. R.E. Clements, 'The Prophecies of Isaiah', pp. 429-33.

98. The shift from third person to second in this fashion is found in Isa. 1.2-4, 24-25, 28-29.

99. There is one other view which merits mention. In Josh. 7.19 we read of an ancient practice in which the condemned person must offer a hymn of praise for the righteousness of God: 'Then Joshua said to Achan, "My son, give glory to the Lord God of Israel, and render praise to him; and tell me now what you have done; do not hide it from me"'. Cf. F. Horst, *ZAW* 47 (1929), pp. 50ff. (as cited in O. Kaiser, *Isaiah 1-12* [OTL; Philadelphia: Westminster Press, 1972], p. 167 in commenting on Isaiah 12). The primary problem with this interesting proposal is that it renders the prophet's reaction inexplicable.

100. W. Rudolph, *Jes. 24-27*, p. 33. Cf. also B. Duhm, *Jesaia*, p. 175; E.J.

Kissane, *Isaiah*, p. 261 who extend the pericope through 25.5. But the stylistic features prevent such a view.

101. In this connection, cf. the discussion of *Angstruf* and *Klageruf* by G.N.M. Habets, *Die grosse Jes.-Apok.*, p. 76.

102. W. Rudolph, *Jes. 24–27*, pp. 31, 32.

103. W.E. March, *Two Prophetic Compositions*, pp. 64, 65.

104. He cites Isa. 48.8; Jer. 3.6-11, 20; 5.11; 9.1; Pss. 78.57; 119.158.

105. H. Wildberger, *Jesaja*, p. 937.

106. *Ibid.*, p. 776; E.J. Young, *Isaiah*, p. 63; G.B. Gray, *Isaiah*, p. 352, citing Dillmann and Cheyne, though he disagrees with their view.

107. CTA, 4.7.29-35. Cf. the discussion of *mrwm* above, p. 35.

108. Cf. B.S. Childs, 'The Enemy from the North and the Chaos Tradition', *JBL* 78 (1959), pp. 187-98, esp. p. 190. He argues that the term *r'š* (v. 18) has become a *terminus technicus* in the literature for the return of chaos.

109. One of the first to suggest this idea was Ibn Ezra who writes that in this pericope *twrt* means, 'The laws which are dictated by common sense, in which all agree'. *ḥq* refers to 'The laws of God contained in the natural order of things' (*The Commentary of Ibn Ezra on Isaiah I*, ed. M. Friedländer [London: Society of Hebrew Literature, 1873], p. 109). According to Gesenius, Vitringa interpreted *twrt* as the 'natural and popular law, not as the positive law' (*Isaiah*, p. 764). This view is followed by W. Rudolph, *Jes. 24–27*, p. 31; G.B. Gray, *Isaiah*, p. 411; R.E. Clements, *Isaiah 1–39*, pp. 201, 202.

110. W. Gesenius, *Isaiah*, p. 764. Cf. also the discussion by H.M. Orlinsky, 'Nationalism—Universalism and Internationalism in Ancient Israel', *Translating and Understanding the Old Testament, Essays in Honor of H.G. May*, ed. H.T. Frank and W. Reed (New York: Abingdon Press). He writes, 'With no people other than Israel did God ever enter into a legally binding relationship' (pp. 213, 214).

111. W. Rudolph (*Jes. 24–27*, p. 31) refers to Ezek. 5.6 as an indication that other nations knew and were held responsible for the law of God. But it is obvious that in this verse the other nations are used by the author as a foil, against which he might emphasize Jerusalem's own disobedience. Similarly, G.B. Gray (*Isaiah*, p. 411) refers to Zech. 9.7 and Ps. 9.18. The first reference is not applicable to this context. Ps. 9.18 reads as follows: 'The wicked shall depart to Sheol, all the nations that forget God'. To equate the 'forgetting' of God by the nations with violation of *twrt* and *ḥq* is simply inappropriate.

112. H. Wildberger, *Jesaja*, p. 922. He bases this conclusion on two things: (1) the fact that the sinaitic covenant is commonly presented with the threat of a curse if it is broken (Lev. 26; Deut. 28 and also Exod. 23.21ff.), just as we have it in v. 6; (2) the terms *twrt* and *ḥq* suggest the sinaitic covenant, though later he denies that these terms *in their present context* suggest any special revelation.

113. *Ibid.*, p. 921. He writes: 'Da, wie immer wieder zu beobachten war, in diesen Abschnitt auch sonst Motive, die Israel betreffen, auf die Erde bzw. deren Bewohner übertragen sind, ist es nicht ausgeschlossen, daß der Verfasser doch nicht nur an den Noahbund denkt, sondern daß er wieder Aussagen von der Menschheit macht, die von Haus aus auf Israel gezielt waren'.

114. *Ibid.*, p. 929.

115. See the development of this argument by J.J.M. Roberts in two forthcoming articles: (1) 'Isaiah and his Children', in a Festschrift for Samuel Iwry, and (2) an article on Isaiah 2 to appear in the *Jewish Quarterly Review*.

116. Note Wildberger's explanation, which is in fact an acknowledgment that his 'Uminterpretation' in this instance is forced : 'Die Einzelexegese hat ergeben, wie stark gerade in diesem Abschnitt überkommene Traditionen Israels aufgenommen sind. Kaum ein Satz, der nicht als Echo von längst ergangenen Prophezeiungen verstanden werden kann. Trotzdem ist das Ganze etwas *völlig anderes* (emphasis mine) als die Summe von Einzelvorstellungen, indem diese dadurch, daß sie auf die "Erde" insgesamt bezogen sind, eine neue Funktion zu übernehmen haben' (*Jesaja*, p. 940).

117. As I noted above, Gesenius and Lowth eliminated the universal dimensions, while most interpreters (Rudolph, Lindblom, Kessler, Plöger, Wildberger, etc.) have excised the particular.

118. M.-L. Henry, *Glaubenskrise*, pp. 133-35.

119. Most interpreters recognize that the concluding unit (vv. 16b-20) reflects the opening verses in scope, though there is a sense of *Steigerung*. Cf. G.N.M. Habets, *Die grosse Jes.-Apok.*, p. 75. He notes that 24.16b-20 is 'parallel' to 24.1-6. This view is also expressed by Lindblom, *Jes.-Apok.*, p. 23; W. Rudolph, *Jes. 24–27*, p. 33.

120. G.N.M. Habets, *ibid.*, pp. 46, 47.

121. There is some debate as to whether this is authentic to Jeremiah. Cf. the review of the literature in B.S. Childs, 'The Enemy from the North', p. 193. J. Bright (*Jeremiah* [AB; New York: Doubleday, 1965], p. 34) presents a convincing case in favor of Jeremianic authorship. Regardless of authorship, it is no later than exilic (with Childs, p. 195), and the literary context indicates that it refers to the devastation of Judah.

122. Cf. the article by W. Brueggemann, 'Weariness, Exile and Chaos', *CBQ* 34 (1972), pp. 19-38, esp. p. 34, where he writes: 'the moment of exile is an experience of chaos'. Also see J.Z. Smith, 'Earth and the Gods', *JR* 49 (1969), pp. 108-27. He notes that the exile is more than a historical event: 'it is above all a thoroughly mythic event: the return to chaos, the decreation, the separation from the deity is analogous to the total catastrophe of the primeval flood' (p. 118).

123. A.J. Wensinck, *Studies of A.J. Wensinck* (New York: Arno Press, 1978), p. 51.

124. *Ibid.*

125. In our introduction we noted an emerging consensus of opinion that Isa. 24–27 should be dated in the sixth century. This view is based on prosodic analysis, lexical studies, and now, our own view that the exile has provided the motivation for this composition.

Notes to Chapter 3

1. It is generally recognized that 24.21–27.1, in its present form, comprises a complete unit.
2. Cf. the title of his dissertation, 'A Study of Two Prophetic Compositions', and particularly pp. 72-75.
3. *Ibid.*
4. Since the discovery of the Ugaritic tablets, the correlation of Isa. 24–27 to this pattern has been recognized by most interpreters. Cf. the extensive discussion by W.R. Millar, *Origin of Apoc.*, pp. 65-102, in which he develops this correlation in great detail.
5. It is strange indeed that March does not perceive this because his understanding of 24.1-20 is similar to my own: it depicts the destruction of Judah.
6. Repetition: 24.22; 26.3, 4, 5, 6, 15; chiasm: 25.3; 26.9b with 10a; inclusio: 24.21, 22 (*pqd*); 25.7, 8 (*bl'*).
7. See the detailed analysis by Millar (*Origin of Apoc.*, pp. 23-61) which supports our position in great detail.
8. P.A. Munch, *The Expression Bajjôm Hahû', Is it an Eschatological Terminus Technicus*? (Oslo: Det Norske Videnskaps-Akademi, 1936).
9. H. Gressmann, *Der Messias* (Göttingen: Vandenhoeck & Ruprecht, 1929), p. 83.
10. P.A. Munch, *The Expression Bajjôm Hahû'*, p. 57.
11. *Ibid.*, pp. 53, 54.
12. J. Barr, *The Semantics of Biblical Language* (Oxford: Oxford University Press, 1961).
13. S.J. DeVries, *Yesterday, Today and Tomorrow* (Grand Rapids: Eerdmans, 1975).
14. I note several other headings and their corresponding references in order to indicate DeVries' methodology and the extensiveness of his approach: (I) Judgment against Israel, expanding judgment against Israel (Isa. 2.20; 3.18; 5.30; 7.18, 20, 23; Hos. 1.5; Amos 8.9, 13); (II) Judgment against the nations, expanding judgment against the nations (Isa. 17.9; 19.16, 19; 23.15; Jer. 25.33; Ezek. 30.9); (III) Judgment against Israel, expanding judgment against the nations (Isa. 17.4); (IV) Salvation, expanding salvation (Isa. 11.1f.; 12.1, 4; Hos. 2.18, 20, 23 [Eng. 2.16, 18, 21]; Joel 4.18 [Eng. 3.18]; Mic. 4.6). See pp. 298-310 for detailed analysis.
15. Cf. the discussion of 29.1-8 in B.S. Childs, *Isaiah and the Assyrian*

Crisis (SBT 3; Naperville, Ill.: Alec R. Allenson, 1967), pp. 53-57. The motif of judgment-deliverance is unmistakable. In this connection, see H. Ringgren, 'Some Observations on Style and Structure in the Isaiah Apocalypse', *ASTI* 9 (1973), pp. 113, 114. He argues convincingly for the existence of the woe-weal pattern, 'destruction and lament are followed by restoration and joy'.

16. S.J. DeVries, *Yesterday, Today and Tomorrow*, p. 298.
17. *Ibid.*, pp. 324, 331.
18. Regarding similarity of style, cf. above, p. 50.
19. O. Plöger, *Theocracy and Eschatology*, p. 59.
20. H. Wildberger, *Jesaja*, pp. 898, 943.
21. Cf. J. Lindblom, *Jes.-Apok.*, p. 26 and O. Kaiser, *Isaiah*, p. 178.
22. O. Plöger, *Theocracy and Eschatology*, p. 60.
23. Ibn Ezra, *Isaiah*, p. 112; B. Duhm, *Jesaia*, p. 177; G.B. Gray, *Isaiah*, p. 423; O. Procksch, *Jesaia*, p. 314; W. Rudolph, *Jes. 24-27*, p. 33; O. Kaiser, *Isaiah*, p. 194.
24. J. Lindblom, *Jes.-Apok.*, p. 27.
25. F. Delitzsch, *Isaiah*, pp. 428, 429.
26. J. Calvin, *Isaiah*, p. 185.
27. H. Wildberger, *Jesaja*, pp. 944-47; W. Kessler, *Gott geht es um das Ganze*, p. 139; M.-L. Henry, *Glaubenskrise*, p. 156; G. Fohrer, *Jesaja*, p. 14; E.J. Kissane, *Isaiah*, p. 283.
28. Cf. the Introduction, pp. 11-14, for an indication of the emerging consensus for an earlier dating of Isa. 24–27. Nowhere in the entirety of the Isaianic corpus does *sb'* suggest angelic beings, nor is there anything in these four chapters or this pericope which would suggest them. The attempt to use the book of Daniel as the interpretive key for Isa. 24–27 is part of the continuing legacy of B. Duhm. With regard to the book of *Enoch*, it is true that the motif of the capture and imprisonment of supernatural beings is present (90.24; 91.15, 54), but in the book of *Enoch* the imagery is much further advanced (cf. the fine discussion by G.W. Anderson, 'Isaiah 24–27', p. 126; while noting the correspondence of ideas, he refers to the thought in Isaiah as 'quite undeveloped'). More is required than similarity of motif in order to substantiate a thesis of synchronal relationship.
29. J.B. Pritchard, *The Ancient Near East, An Anthology of Texts and Pictures* I (Princeton: Princeton University Press, 1969), p. 34. Cf. E.J. Kissane, *Isaiah*, p. 283.
30. Cf. J. Day, '*tl 'wrt* in Isa. 26.19', *ZAW* 90 (1978), pp. 267, 268. Of importance is Day's argumentation that this is stereotypical language related to the enthronement of Yahweh. Therefore it is unnecessary to see behind the 'hosts' and 'kings' several other nations. As the following pericope (25.1-5) demonstrates, there is but one enemy which must be destroyed.
31. F. Delitzsch, *Isaiah*, p. 430; J. Lindblom, *Jes.-Apok.*, p. 30; O. Kaiser,

Isaiah, p. 195. But cf. M.A. Klopfenstein, *Scham und Schande nach dem Alten Testament* (AThANT 62; 1972), p. 82.

32. H. Wildberger, *Jesaja*, p. 947. I would not deny that there is an intended contrast between the brightness of Yahweh's glory over against the shining of the sun and moon. I simply note that the polemic against these two heavenly bodies is usually missed. Wildberger's point is well taken.

33. J. Calvin, *Isaiah*, p. 186.

34. J. Lindblom, *Jes.-Apok.*, p. 28.

35. M.-L. Henry, *Glaubenskrise*, p. 159. She designates the phrase as 'an admonition to patience'; it is an acknowledgment that pushes the time of Shalom into the future.

36. S. Mowinckel, *The Psalms in Israel's Worship* (trans. by D.R. Ap-Thomas, New York: Abingdon Press, 1962); G. von Rad, 'The Origin of the Concept of the Day of Yahweh', *JSS* 4 (1959), pp. 97-108; H.-J. Kraus, *Die Königsherrschaft Gottes im Alten Testament* (BHT 13; Tübingen: J.C. Mohr, 1951). Cf. the excellent summary of views in J. Gray, 'The Day of Yahweh in Cultic Experience and Eschatological Perspective', *SEÅ* 39 (1974), pp. 5-37. This subject is discussed at length in several of the commentaries, but see particularly H. Wildberger, *Jesaja*, pp. 947-49 and G.N.M. Habets, *Die grosse Jes.-Apok.*, pp. 226-37 and his excursus, pp. 334ff.

37. This supports our understanding of 24.1-20 as a depiction of the destruction of Jerusalem which results in the exile of both God and people. Cf. the quotation of Wensinck, p. 47 above.

38. P. Hanson, *Dawn*, p. 212.

39. Most interpreters appear not to know what to do with this phrase. But cf. O. Kaiser, *Isaiah*, p. 195, for support of my interpretation.

40. J. Lindblom, *Jes.-Apok.*, p. 30; O. Kaiser, *Isaiah*, p. 197: W. Rudolph, *Jes. 24–27*, p. 34; H. Wildberger, *Jesaja*, p. 899.

41. P. Lohmann, 'Die selbständigen lyrischen Abschnitte in Jes. 24–27', *ZAW* 37 (1917), pp. 1-58, see p. 16. See the extended discussion of the *Gattung* of this pericope in P.L. Redditt, *Isaiah 24–27*, pp. 106-15.

42. *Ibid.*

43. H. Wildberger, *Jesaja*, p. 953.

44. *Ibid.*

45. O. Plöger, *Theocracy and Eschatology*, p. 69. On p. 71 Plöger writes: 'The two psalms, 25.1 and 26.1 . . . need not be referred to in interpreting the eschatological narrative, which forms the central portion of these chapters'. This methodology of interpretation can only be distortive of the comprehensive picture which the author (or even editor) has created.

46. B. Duhm, *Jesaia*, p. 172. He credits Ewald and Smend for their earlier 'contributions' in this area, p. 179.

47. W. Rudolph, *Jes. 24–27*, p. 34. Rudolph is supported by M.-L. Henry who refers to v. 3 as 'den notwendigen Zwischengedanken . . . der die

Teilnahme "Aller Völker" am eschatologischen Freudenmahl begründe' (*Glaubenskrise*, pp. 183, 184).

48. *Ibid*., p. 35. He concludes that the author of 25.1-5 and the author of 24.1-23 are one and the same. In addition to the points which I mentioned above, he notes the similarity of style: (a) the juxtaposition of like-sounding words in v. 1b as in 24.16, 17; (b) the word play, *zrm*, *zrym*, *zmyr*, in vv. 4 and 5 as in 24.1, 3, 4. Similarly, W.R. Millar (*Origin of Apoc*., p. 43) concludes on the basis of stylistic considerations that the same author was responsible for 24.1–25.9. These are significant points, and should caution against the hasty assignment of the literature to different authors.

49. O. Kaiser, *Isaiah*, p. 197, though a word of caution is in order due to Kaiser's propensity for seeing apocalyptic, end-time allusions in the most unexpected places.

50. *Ibid*., pp. 197, 198. Cf. G. Fohrer, *Jesaja*, pp. 16, 17. It may be argued that since hymns normally refer to past events, then so must this hymn. But against this view, three objections may be raised: (1) A careful analysis of the hymn reveals a future orientation, as Kaiser has indicated. (2) The immediate context refers to a day in the future when Yahweh will reign and provide an eschatological banquet. At this point, Wildberger is correct in stressing that regardless of origin, 'in its present context', the hymn must be regarded as referring to a future event. (3) The greater context, particularly the lament in 26.7-18 suggests that the deliverance has not yet come. This certainly would be inexplicable if Yahweh had already defeated the enemy power.

51. In this matter, the author is operating with a view similar to that of Second Isaiah, who saw the future overthrow of Babylon as the initial act of the new age. Cf. the excellent essay which highlights this aspect in Second Isaiah's thought: B.W. Anderson, 'Exodus Typology in Second Isaiah', *Israel's Prophetic Heritage, Essays in Honor of James Muilenburg*, ed. B.W. Anderson, W. Harrelson (New York: Harper and Brothers, 1962), pp. 177-95.

52. B. Duhm, *Jesaia*, p. 179. Duhm maintained that this psalm celebrated the destruction of Samaria by John Hyrcanus between 111 and 107 BCE.

53. O. Procksch, *Jesaia*, pp. 345, 346. The destruction of Carthage by C. Scipio Aemilanus in 146 was Procksch's view.

54. O. Eissfeldt, *Introduction*, p. 326. He proposed the third century for the overthrow of a Moabite city. Rudolph concurs with my point: '... darf man in ihr (the city) die Repräsentantin des Weltreichs oder der Weltreiche sehen. Damit scheiden Samaria, Tyrus, Sidon, Karthago aus' (*Jes. 24–27*, p. 62).

55. J. Bright, *Jeremiah*, p. 359.

56. M.-L. Henry, *Glaubenskrise*, pp. 20-34.

57. J. Lindblom, *Jes.-Apoc*., pp. 72f., followed by W. Kessler, *Gott geht es um das Ganze*, p. 142, and G.W. Anderson, 'Isaiah 24–27', pp. 118ff.

58. W. Rudolph, *Jes. 24–27*, p. 62.

59. See my refutation of this, pp. 31f. above.

60. J. Bright, *Jeremiah*, p. 360. Cf. also Wildberger's comment regarding Isaiah 13 that it was composed several years prior to 539, 'als Reaktion auf die noch nicht lange zurückliegende Eroberung Jerusalems durch Nebukadnezar' (*Jesaia*, p. 511).

61. It is generally agreed that the terms *dl* and *'bywn* are *termini technici* for the Jewish community in the exilic and post-exilic eras. J.J.M. Roberts has correctly noted that 25.4 is a re-interpretation of an earlier motif from First Isaiah who held that such protection of the poor and needy was the responsibility of the kings and princes. In the new age, Yahweh will be the protection of his people ('Isaiah in Old Testament Theology', *Interpretation* 36 [1982], p. 142). Cf. also Isa. 40.11; 41.17-20 which highlight Yahweh's similar role, which may suggest that this was a particularly exilic motif.

62. O. Plöger, *Theocracy and Eschatology*, p. 62; M.-L. Henry, *Glaubenskrise*, pp. 184f.; H. Wildberger, *Jesaja*, p. 971.

63. J. DeVries, *Yesterday, Today and Tomorrow*, p. 302.

64. O. Procksch, *Jesaia*, p. 319.

65. J. Lindblom, *Jes.-Apok.*, p. 34.

66. The consistent meter supports this idea, and there is no compelling reason for attributing this to a later editor.

67. Cf. Isa. 18.7; 45.14; 60.3; Ps. 72.10.

68. H. Wildberger, *Jesaja*, p. 961.

69. J.F. Stenning, *The Targum of Isaiah*, pp. 78, 79; also cited by G.B. Gray, *Isaiah*, p. 429.

70. P.L. Redditt, *Isaiah 24–27*, pp. 213, 214; cf. also p. 360. His remarks are directed primarily against M.-L. Henry, who may be guilty on other occasions of excising those portions which do not seem to fit her universalistic pattern (e.g. cf. her discussion of 27.2-11, *Glaubenskrise*, pp. 196-99), but who is basically correct regarding 25.6-10a.

71. This phrase is employed in another context by R. Davidson, but is applicable here ('Universalism in Second Isaiah', *SJT* 16 [1963], p. 181).

72. See the discussion on this matter by D.G. Johnson, 'The Structure and Meaning of Romans 11', *CBQ* 46 (1984), pp. 91-103.

73. This is likewise the thrust of 25.1-3. Yahweh's defeat of Israel's enemy will result in the conversion of the nations. Note that the pattern of Exile—Deliverance—Conversion of the Nations, is well known from Second Isaiah.

74. W. Rudolph, *Jes. 24–27*, p. 40; J. Lindblom, *Jes.-Apok.*, p. 37; O. Plöger, *Theocracy and Eschatology*, p. 61.

75. *Ibid.*

76. O. Plöger, *Theocracy and Eschatology*, p. 61.

77. J.K.W. Vatke, *Die Biblische Theologie wissenschaftlich dargestellt* (Berlin: G. Bethge Verlag, 1835), pp. 500, 501. In accordance with Hegelian

idealism, Vatke believed that the conquering of Judah, the destruction of the temple and the exile to Babylon, as tragic as these events were, had the affect of removing the physical trappings and allowing the fuller expression of the Absolute Spirit.

78. M.-L. Henry, *Glaubenskrise*, p. 153.
79. *Ibid*, p. 164.
80. F. Delitzsch, *Isaiah*, p. 434; O. Procksch, *Jesaia*, p. 319.
81. W. Rudolph, *Jes. 24–27*, p. 39; G.B. Gray, *Isaiah*, p. 430; J. Lindblom, *Jes.-Apok*., pp. 37, 38; G. Fohrer, *Jesaja*, p. 20; W. Kessler, *Gott geht es um das Ganze*, p. 144; H. Wildberger, *Jesaja*, p. 966.
82. B. Duhm, *Jesaia*, p. 181; J. Lindblom, *Jes.-Apok*., p. 36; O. Kaiser, *Isaiah*, p. 199; O. Plöger, *Theocracy and Eschatology*, p. 61.
83. *Ibid*.
84. W.R. Millar, *Origin of Apoc*., pp. 41, 42.
85. *Ibid*.
86. O. Kaiser, *Isaiah*, p. 199.
87. *Ibid*., p. 201.
88. O. Plöger, *Theocracy and Eschatology*, p. 61.
89. *CTA* 5.2.2-4, based in part on *CTA* 23.61-64.
90. H. Wildberger, *Jesaja*, p. 967.
91. This argumentation is supported by Wildberger: 'Von Auferstehung spricht der Text nicht, wohl aber davon, daß Jahwes Heilswillen keine Grenzen mehr gesetzt sind'. To be sure, as Wildberger affirms, the later belief in the resurrection from the dead finds its initial impetus with the greater concept of the unrestricted reign of Yahweh, which is the thrust of 25.6-10a, but with an added dimension from Iranian religion (*Jesaja*, p. 967). See also the helpful discussion in C. Barth, *Introduction to the Psalms* (trans. R.A. Wilson; New York, Charles Scribner's Sons, 1966), pp. 49-55. He correctly maintains that in the Psalms *mwt* refers to an anti-godly power.
92. Cf. Jer. 23.40; 24.9; 29.18; 42.18; 44.8, 12; Lam. 5.1; Ezek. 5.14, 15; 16.57; 22.14; 36.15, 30; Pss. 44.14; 79.4; 89.42; also Neh. 2.17; Isa. 54.4.
93. H. Wildberger, *Jesaja*, p. 968.
94. O. Kaiser, *Isaiah*, p. 201.
95. G.B. Gray, *Isaiah*, p. 431.
96. O. Plöger, *Theocracy and Eschatology*, p. 62.
97. Cf. Isa. 1.25; 11.11, 15; 19.16; 31.3; 34.17; 40.2; 43.13; 48.13; 49.2, 22; 50.2, 11; 51.16, 17; 59.1; 62.3; 66.2.
98. E.J. Young, *Isaiah*, p. 199.
99. Most scholars agree that 25.10b-12 is a later addition to the text.
100. B. Duhm, *Jesaia*, p. 183; G.B. Gray, *Isaiah*, p. 437.
101. P. Lohmann, 'Die selbständigen lyrischen Abschnitte', p. 38.
102. *Ibid*., p. 7.
103. *Ibid*., p. 16.
104. J. Lindblom, *Jes.-Apok*., pp. 40f.

105. O. Kaiser, *Isaiah*, p. 205; W. Rudolph, *Jes. 24–27*, pp. 42, 43; O. Plöger, *Theocracy and Eschatology*, p. 69; W. Kessler, *Gott geht es um das Ganze*, p. 149; G. Fohrer, *Jesaja*, pp. 22f.; H. Wildberger, *Jesaja*, p. 976; P.L. Redditt, *Isaiah 24–27*, pp. 122f.; W.E. March, *Two Prophetic Compositions*, p. 116.

106. B. Duhm, *Jesaia*, p. 183.

107. G.B. Gray, *Isaiah*, p. 437.

108. Cf. W. Rudolph, *Jes. 24–27*, p. 42.

109. W.E. March, *Two Prophetic Compositions*, p. 122.

110. J. Lindblom, *Jes.-Apok.*, p. 40; P.L. Redditt, *Isaiah 24–27*, p. 124.

111. P. Lohmann, 'Die selbständigen lyrischen Abschnitte', p. 38.

112. H. Wildberger, *Jesaja*, pp. 904, 976.

113. Because DeVries fails to recognize the intrusive nature of 25.10b-12, he regards 26.1-6 as an expansion of the judgment against Moab, *Yesterday, Today and Tomorrow*, pp. 305, 306. But with the excision of vv. 10b-12, 26.1-6 is properly seen as a continuation of the expression of trust in 25.9-10a.

114. I am indebted to O. Kaiser (*Isaiah*, p. 206) who notes, 'It should be particularly emphasized that within the song the call to praise and thanksgiving is replaced by a call to trust in Yahweh'.

115. H. Wildberger, *Jesaja*, p. 978.

116. On the subject of the rebuilding of the walls of the city of Jerusalem, see J. Lindblom's discussion (*Jes.-Apok.*, pp. 85-90). His critique of other positions is incisive, but he errs in regarding it as a past event.

117. The logic is similar to that of Isa. 40.1-31: the announcement of an imminent deliverance (vv. 1-11) is followed by an affirmation of Yahweh's ability to effect the promised deliverance (12-26). But because the deliverance lies in the future, while the community continues in a sorry state (note the disputation in v. 27), it is necessary to follow with an expression of trust (vv. 28-31).

118. W.R. Millar, *Origin of Apoc.*, p. 85.

119. Cf. Millar's excellent discussion on this, pp. 85ff.

120. But see the substantive critique by D. Hillers, 'Ritual Procession of the Ark and Psalm 132', *CBQ* 30 (1968), p. 48. He maintains that Ps. 132.8 cannot be used as evidence for the use of the ark in the cultic practice of a ritual procession; see his conclusion, p. 52.

121. In my judgment, the processional language in v. 2, located as it is in a pericope which is designed to encourage those who are suffering oppression and who doubt that there will be any deliverance, is reminiscent of Second Isaiah's promise to the exiles that they would return to Jerusalem on a high and holy way (40.3-5, 11, 31; 42.16; 52.7-12; 55.12).

122. O. Kaiser, *Isaiah*, p. 207. Calvin's comment on this is worthy of note: 'You have no reason for being terrified at the greatness or strength of Babylon: for she will quickly fall, and will not stand before the power of the Lord' (*Isaiah*, p. 216).

123. O. Eissfeldt, *Introduction*, p. 324.

124. W. Rudolph, *Jes. 24–27*, pp. 6-8, 42f.; W. Kessler, *Gott geht es um das Ganze*, pp. 153ff.

125. J. Lindblom, *Jes.-Apok.*, pp. 40ff.

126. W. Rudolph, *Jes. 24–27*, pp. 42ff.

127. J. Lindblom, *Jes.-Apok.*, p. 41.

128. H. Gunkel, *Einleitung in die Psalmen* (Göttingen: Vandenhoeck & Ruprecht, 1933), p. 117.

129. J. Lindblom, *Jes.-Apok.*, pp. 41, 42.

130. *Ibid.*

131. *Ibid.*, p. 64.

132. By eliminating all of the occurrences of *bywm hhw'* as secondary additions, Lindblom has decided to interpret a text other than the one which is a part of the Isaianic tradition.

133. H. Wildberger, *Jesaja*, p. 987.

134. Rather than treating the verbs as simple past, it is to be noted that it is a common practice in lament forms to express a plea in the precative mood. Cf. Pss. 10.16; 31.6; 57.7; 116.6; Job 21.16; 22.18; Lam. 1.21; 3.57-61.

135. Cf. Prov. 2.20-22; 3.6; 4.18; 15.19.

136. Note also the Exodus tradition which suggests that the revealing of the *name* is the catalyst for the ensuing acts of deliverance (Exod. 3.5).

137. Cf. the excellent discussion by H.H. Schmid, 'Schöpfung, Gerechtigkeit und Heil, "Schöpfungstheólogie" als Gesamthorizont biblischer Theologie', *ZThK* (1970), pp. 1-19; ET 'Creation, Righteousness and Salvation, "Creation Theology" as the Broad Horizon of Biblical Theology', *Creation in the Old Testament*, ed. B.W. Anderson (Philadelphia: Fortress Press, 1984).

138. *Ibid.*

139. W. Kessler, *Gott geht es um das Ganze*, p. 152.

140. See especially his *Dawn*.

141. *Ibid.*, p. 314.

142. O. Plöger, *Theocracy and Eschatology*, pp. 65, 66.

143. *Ibid.*, p. 65.

144. Cf. our reading of *qn't-'m* as 'antagonists of the people' rather than the common translation, 'zeal for your people' which makes little sense. M. Dahood first proposed this reading on the basis of Ps. 119.139. See his discussion in *Psalms III* (AB; Garden City, NY: Doubleday, 1970), pp. 189, 190.

145. Note that this is the same relationship that we observed in 25.1-10a: The destruction of the enemy would lead to a situation of *Heil*.

146. LXX reads *panta gar apedōkas hēmin*, but this is not helpful since the key term, *apedōkas*, may have either a positive or a negative connotation.

147. H. Wildberger, *Jesaja*, p. 991.

148. G.B. Gray, *Isaiah*, pp. 443f., O. Plöger, *Theocracy and Eschatology*,

p. 67; H. Wildberger, *Jesaja*, pp. 991f., E.J. Kissane, *Isaiah*, p. 296; W. Rudolph, *Jes. 24–27*, p. 47.

149. Cf. W. Holladay's discussion of these verses and his reasoning which is similar to my own (*Isaiah*, p. 203).

150. Cf. W. Kessler's comment: 'Fremdherrschaft über Israel wirkte sich aus als Herrschaftanspruch fremder Götter' (*Gott geht es um as Ganze*, p. 156). Note also the recent discussion on a related subject by H. Spieckermann, *Juda unter Assur in der Sargonzeit* (Göttingen: Vandenhoeck & Ruprecht, 1982).

151. Cf. the parallel role of Ps. 44.18-21 in that lament. Note *nzkyr šmk* and *'m-škḥnw šm*.

152. Cf. Pss. 6.5f.; 30.10ff.; 88.11ff.; and Isa. 38.17f.; also H. Wildberger's discussion of death in the thinking of the ancient Near East is particularly helpful (*Jesaja*, p. 992).

153. Note the reiteration of *mtym*, *wḥyw*, *yqwmw*.

154. *mwsr* is used frequently in the OT as a reference to the exile (cf. Isa. 53.5; Jer. 7.28; 17.23; 30.14, 17; Ezek. 5.15; Deut. 11.2).

155. The Hebrew *npl* may carry the idea of childbirth, as an infant 'falls' from its mother in birth.

156. C. Westermann, *Isaiah 40–66*

157. *Ibid.*

158. W.R. Millar, *Origin of Apoc.*, p. 114: 'The author (of Isa. 24–27) emerges as one very much influenced by the work of Second Isaiah'. P. Hanson (*Dawn*, p. 313) attributes the authorship of the 'Isaiah Apocalypse' to a 'disciple of Second Isaiah'.

159. O. Kaiser, *Isaiah*, pp. 215-20.

160. H. Gunkel, *Die Psalmen*, p. 137, though he includes vv. 20, 21 as well; W. Rudolph, *Jes. 24–27*, pp. 23, 48; J. Lindblom, *Jes.-Apok.*, p. 50; O. Plöger, *Theocracy and Eschatology*, p. 67; H. Wildberger, *Jesaja*, pp. 994f.

161. C. Westermann, *Praise and Lament in the Psalms* (Atlanta: John Knox Press, 1981; first German edn, 1961), p. 61.

162. H. Wildberger, *Jesaja*, p. 995. I cite O. Kaiser as but one example of the several extraordinary attempts to lay aside v. 19 as a later interpolation: '(v. 19) can be seen from v. 20 to be a later interpolation (which) first stood in the margin in a rather unclear form and was later copied in different ways. (In the footnote he continues) If v. 10 were original, it would conflict with v. 20 in its original meaning, because the hope of v. 19 would overshadow the advice on how to behave during the final stress' (p. 216). Kaiser's proposal belongs with those other futile attempts so aptly described by Preuss: 'Die in der bisherigen Forschung zum Text vorliegenden zahlreichen Umstellungs-, Teilungs- und Streichungsvorschläge ermuntern geradezu, es zu versuchen, den Text einmal wieder wie vorliegend zu interpretieren' (quoted by H. Wildberger, *Jesaja*, p. 995).

163. W. Rudolph, *Jes. 24–27*, p. 48. Note that some of the specific imagery

in Ezekiel 37 corresponds precisely with Isa. 26.19: 'Behold, I will *open your graves* and *raise you from your graves*, O my people' (Ezek. 37.12).

164. Cf. in the larger scriptural tradition: Lam. 3.6; Hos. 13.14.

165. J.Z. Smith, 'Earth and Gods', p. 119.

166. On the meaning of the phrase, *tl 'wrt*, see the superb discussion by J. Day, '*tl 'wrt* in Isaiah 26.19', *ZAW* 90 (1978), pp. 265-69. He regards the phrase as an allusion to the national resurrection. Cf. Hos. 6.23; Ps. 110.3.

167. H. Wildberger, *Jesaja*, p. 998; G. Fohrer, *Jesaja*, p. 32; W. Kessler, *Gott geht es um das Ganze*, p. 159; O. Procksch, *Jesaja*, p. 333; view v. 20 as a reference to the flood. But cf. G.B. Gray, *Isaiah*, p. 449; Fischer and Ziegler (cited by Kaiser, *Isaiah*, p. 214), who support the Exodus tradition.

168. *Contra* J. Lindblom, *Jes.-Apok.*, p. 52, who suggested that *ḥdr* meant 'grave', cf. Gen. 43.30; Judg. 16.9; Exod. 7.28; 1 Sam. 4.7.

169. H. Wildberger, *Jesaja*, p. 998.

170. Earlier critical scholars viewed 27.1 as a reference to three separate kingdoms, but with the discovery of the mythological texts from Ugarit, there can be no doubt that the various descriptions within the verse refer to the one chaos monster. This material has been widely discussed and is readily available in the commentaries so that it is unnecessary to discuss it further here. Cf. the fine discussion by H. Wildberger, *Jesaja*, pp. 1001-1006.

171. See the discussion by E.M. McGuire, 'Yahweh and Leviathan: An Exegesis of Isaiah 27.1', *RQ* 13 (1970), pp. 165-79.

172. S.J. DeVries, *Yesterday, Today and Tomorrow*, pp. 314-23. He lists other passages in which *bywn hhw'* functions as a concluding formula: Isa. 10.27; 20.6; 31.7; 52.6; Jer. 4.9; Amos 2.16; 8.3; Obad. 8; Hag. 2.23; Zech. 9.16; 12.4; 14.21.

173. *Ibid*. Definition as given in DeVries' glossary, p. 353.

Notes to Chapter 4

1. G.B. Gray, *Isaiah*, p. 453; E.J. Kissane, *Isaiah*, pp. 292, 299; W.E. March, *Two Prophetic Compositions*, p. 189; W. Holladay, *Isaiah*, p. 206.

2. P. Lohmann, 'Die selbständigen lyrischen Abschnitte', p. 37; B. Duhm, *Jesaia*, pp. 189, 190; F. Delitzsch, *Isaiah*, pp. 453, 454; H. Wildberger, *Jesaja*, pp. 1007, 1012; O. Kaiser, *Isaiah*, p. 224; P.L. Redditt, *Isa. 24–27*, pp. 137, 138.

3. J. Lindblom, *Jes.-Apok.*, p. 53.

4. O. Kaiser, *Isaiah*, p. 224.

5. J. Lindblom, *Jes.-Apok.*, p. 54. Lindblom wants to see the city in 27.10 as Babylon, and therefore he is eager to connect the negative thrust of vv. 7-11 with the positive song in vv. 2-6 in such a way that it would appear that the Jewish community rejoices in the song of the vineyard because the

enemy has been destroyed in vv. 7-11. In addition to the fact that the city in vv. 7-11 cannot be Babylon, the break after v. 6 will not allow Lindblom's schema.

6. *Ibid*. Lindblom thinks that the song bespeaks the same happy situation as the other songs do. Therefore he concludes: 'Under these circumstances, the introductory words, *bywm hhw'*, cannot be part of the original poem'. But this is to allow one's interpretation to determine the text. Cf. also W. Rudolph, *Jes. 24–27*, p. 52; O. Procksch, *Jesaia*, p. 337; O. Plöger, *Theocracy and Eschatology*, p. 71.

7. Cf. especially, E. Jacob, 'Du premier au deuxième chant de la vigne du prophète Esaïe. Réflexions sur Esaïe 27.2-5', *Wort—Gebot—Glaube, Beiträge zur Theologie des Alten Testaments, Walter Eichrodt zum 80. Geburtstag*, ed. J.J. Stamm, E. Jenni, H.J. Stoebe (AThANT 59; Zürich: Zwingli Verlag, 1970), pp. 325-30; G. Fohrer, *Jesaja*, pp. 36, 37; H. Wildberger, *Jesaja*, pp. 1008, 1009.

8. G.B. Gray, *Isaiah*, p. 453; E.J. Kissane, *Isaiah*, p. 300; J. Lindblom, *Jes.-Apok.*, p. 55; E.J. Young, *Isaiah* p. 240; O. Plöger, *Theocracy and Eschatology*, p. 72.

9. O. Kaiser, *Isaiah*, p. 225; cf. Isa. 10.17 for *šmyr* and *šyt* as representing an external enemy. Also H. Wildberger, *Jesaja*, p. 1011.

10. W. Kessler, *Gott geht es um das Ganze*, p. 167; H. Wildberger, *Jesaja*, p. 1011.

11. Scholars are generally agreed that v. 6 is a clear attempt to include the erstwhile Northern kingdom. Cf. G.B. Gray, *Isaiah*, p. 455; O. Kaiser, *Isaiah*, p. 226; O. Plöger, *Theocracy and Eschatology*, p. 73; E.J. Kissane, *Isaiah*, p. 301; W. Kessler, *Gott geht es um das Ganze*, p. 168.

12. Zimmerli attributes Ezek. 37.15-23 and the theme of reunification to the prophet Ezekiel, *Ezekiel 2* (trans. by J.O. Martin; Hermeneia; Philadelphia: Fortress Press, 1983), p. 272. Bright thinks that Jeremiah 31 is a collection of Jeremiah's oracles which he gave during the time of Josiah's northward expansion, but which were edited no later than the exile (*Jeremiah*, pp. 284, 285). Certainly this evidence does not require that Isa. 27.2ff. be contemporaneous with these exilic writings, but it does demonstrate that the motif of reunification was prevalent at this time. My point is that there is nothing that requires that the theme of reunification be as late as the Samaritan schism.

13. Cf. W. Rudolph, *Jes. 24–27*, p. 53: 'Dies ist der schwierigste Abschnitt in Kap. 24–27'. P. Lohmann, 'Die selbständigen lyrischen Abschnitte', p. 27: these verses 'gehören zu den schwierigsten der Gesamtapokalypse'. B. Duhm (*Jesaia*, p. 191) notes that a section 'ist reich an Schwierigkeiten'. O. Kaiser (*Isaiah*, p. 226) entitles this portion, 'A Difficult Text'. And W. Holladay (Isaiah, p. 206) states that 'verses 2-11 are quite obscure... (therefore) we must confess our uncertainty of the direction of the passage'.

14. B. Duhm, *Jesaia*, p. 191.
15. E.J. Kissane, *Isaiah*, p. 302; W. Rudolph, *Jes. 24–27*, p. 26.
16. Among those interpreters who maintain that 27.10 refers to a foreign city are J. Lindblom, *Jes.-Apok.*, pp. 58, 72ff. (Babylon); O. Procksch, *Jesaia*, pp. 342, 346 (Carthage); E. Kissane, *Isaiah*, p. 302 (Assyria).
17. Those who interpret the city as Samaria are W. Kessler, *Gott geht es um das Ganze*, p. 170; H. Wildberger, *Jesaja*, pp. 1019, 1020; O. Plöger, *Theocracy and Eschatology*, p. 74.
18. The city is identified as Jerusalem by W. Gesenius, *Jesaia*, p. 820; F. Delitzsch, *Isaiah*, p. 456; J. Calvin, *Isaiah*, pp. 252, 253; B. Duhm, *Jesaja*, pp. 192, 193; E.J. Young, *Isaiah*, pp. 247, 248; W. Rudolph, *Jes. 24–27*, pp. 53-55; R. Hahnhart, 'Die jahwefeindliche Stadt', pp. 153-56.
19. Cf. the comment by O. Kaiser: 'In fact almost every argument in favour of identification with any one city can be countered by an argument in favour of another' (*Isaiah*, p. 230).
20. J. Vermeylen, *La composition littéraire de l'apocalypse d'Isaïe (Is., XXIV–XXVII)* (ALBO Ser. V; Fasc. 14, 1974), pp. 33-35. This point was also made independently by J.J.M. Roberts in conversation.
21. Since *'šrym* and *ḥmnym* are also mentioned in Ezek. 6.4, 6, it is by no means necessary to assume that they can only be post-exilic. Further we have archaeological evidence of these cult objects dating back to the tenth/ninth centuries; cf. J. Pritchard, *The Ancient Near East*, illustration no. 148. This evidence also undermines those scholars who would place Isa. 17.8 late because of the similar reference (e.g. O. Kaiser, *Isaiah*, pp. 82-83). Cf. also Lev. 26.30; 2 Chron. 14.2ff.; 34.3ff., and for a detailed discussion of the *'šrym* and *ḥmnym*, cf. J. Lindblom, *Jes.-Apok.*, pp. 118ff.
22. Nearly all interpreters agree that Yahweh is the subject here. Interestingly, Delitzsch understands the verse as, 'Has Yahweh slain Israel as harshly as Israel's enemy has slain Israel?' (*Isaiah*, p. 454). But cf. our translation of this verse in the Appendix.
23. Cf. Hos. 13.15; 12.2. Kaiser is alone in denying an allegorical interpretation, maintaining that it is a reference to an actual storm sent by Yahweh. But the other allusions to exile, along with the mention of the destruction of the city, argue against Kaiser (cf. his *Isaiah*, p. 227).
24. Cf. O. Kaiser, *Isaiah*, p. 228, who notes that the use of the term *šlh*, with its related image of driving out a woman, 'assumes that there was a particularly close relation between the city and Yahweh' (cf. Isa. 50.1). Such references to the exile, along with the language of v. 11b ('a people without understanding', 'their maker', and 'their creator'), have led most interpreters to conclude that the author could not be referring to a foreign city. Further, those who understand 27.10 to be a foreign city, identical with the city in 25.2 and 26.5, 6 must be troubled by the lack of celebration in 27.10. Lohmann, in an imaginative attempt to circumvent this problem, proposed that the opening portion of the 'song of celebration' was lost so that only a

torso remained ('Die selbständigen lyrischen Abschnitte', pp. 27, 28). No one has seconded this view.

25. The phrase, *kl-pry*, is problematic. It never occurs elsewhere in the Hebrew Bible, and it simply makes no sense in this context. I have proposed the following reading: *wzh kl kprw hsr ht'tw*, 'And this will be his full ransom to remove his sin'. The initial *kaph* on *kprw* was mistakenly regarded as a *yod*, a common occurrence. This suggestion requires no deletion of a word and provides a nicely balanced line.

26. Though cf. Hos. 10.2b, where we read that Yahweh is the subject. R. Hahnhart regards v. 9a as an interpretive interjection, with vv. 8, 9b, 10 as statements describing Yahweh's punitive action against Judah. But in the light of the conditional aspect suggested by *bz't*, and the reference in 17.8 in which the people of Israel are the agents, Hahnhart's view regarding v. 9a, 9b seems improbable. See his 'die jahwefeindliche Stadt', pp. 161, 162.

27. Cf. Isa. 41.8; 42.2; 43.1-3, 22; 44.1, 2, 5, 21; 45.3; 48.1, 12; Jer. 30.18; 31.11, 12; Lam. 1.17; 2.1, 2, 5.

28. In Jer. 49.31 there is a reference to the city, Keder, that is *bdd*. However, the usage there is quite different from the usage in Isa. 27.10 or Lam. 1.1. The reference in Jer. 49.31 is to city that 'dwells secure'.

29. Cf. the phrase, *mnhr mṣrym 'd hnhr hgdl nhr prt* in Gen. 15.18; Exod. 23.31; Deut. 1.7; Josh. 1.4.

30. I recognize that the conditional sense which I have stated is not in v. 11b. I am interpreting this verse in the greater context of the entire pericope which does convey a sense of conditionality (cf. v. 9). Also, one might argue that v. 11b is a straightforward prediction of judgment. But one must recognize that v. 10 implies that the city already lies in ruins (cf. also vv. 7, 8 which refer to a past action).

31. W. Kessler, *Gott geht es um das Ganze*, pp. 168-70.

32. H. Wildberger, *Jesaja*, pp. 1016, 1017.

33. *Ibid*. pp. 1017, 1018.

34. O. Plöger, *Theocracy and Eschatology*, p. 73.

35. The text in Ezekiel is unclear as to whether or not Judah is included with Ephraim in the warning against idolatry.

36. We mentioned the terms, *qdym*, *bdd*, *'zb*, *mdbr*, *bṣwrh*.

37. B. Duhm, *Jesaia*, p. 193; O. Kaiser, *Isaiah*, p. 231; G.B. Gray, *Isaiah*, p. 461, who quotes Marti approvingly: 'Yahweh institutes a great threshing, the Jews are the good corn, the heathen the straw. The Jews are picked up one by one, the heathen removed'; H. Wildberger, *Jesaja*, p. 1023.

38. O. Kaiser, *Isaiah*, p. 231.

39. Cf. Judg. 6.11; Deut. 24.20; Ruth 2.17.

40. Cf. Exod. 16.4, 18, 22; Num. 11.8; Ruth 2.8; Ps. 104.28; Gen. 31.46; Cant. 6.2; and especially Isa. 17.5.

41. This is also the view of W. Gesenius, *Jesaia*, pp. 821, 822; F. Delitzsch, *Isaiah*, p. 457; E.J. Kissane, *Isaiah*, p. 303. Certainly this would greatly

undermine any view that was based on a reference to wheat and chaff.

42. Cf. Jer. 4.5, 19, 21; 6.1, 17; Hos. 5.8; 8.1; Joel 2.1; Amos 3.6; Zeph. 1.16; Ezek. 33.4, 5.

43. Cf. Exod. 19.19; 20.18; Josh. 6.6, 13.

44. Cf. Joel 2.15; Ps. 81.4; also G. Fohrer, *Jesaja*, p. 38.

45. B. Duhm, *Jesaia*, p. 193, correctly ascribes this connotation to the terms, *h'bdym* and *hndḥym*.

46. H. Wildberger, *Jesaja*, p. 1024.

47. B. Duhm, *Jesaia*, pp. 189ff. Cf. also W. Holladay (*Isaiah*, p. 206): 'The rest of chapter 27 consists of various additions to the basic apocalyptic collection'; O. Kaiser (*Isaiah*, p. 224): '27.2-6 is the first of a whole series of additions'; G.B. Gray (*Isaiah*, p. 457): 'The connection of these verses (7-11) with what precedes and with what follows is loose, and they probably formed no original part . . . of the apocalypse'; O. Plöger (*Theocracy and Eschatology*, pp. 71, 75): 'The separate parts of chap. 27 can only be supplementary—of very varied character'. 'We can confidently regard ch. 27 as an addition which does not contribute very much to the interpretation of the eschatological narrative in chs. 24–26'; W. Kessler, *Gott geht es um das Ganze*, p. 164; H. Wildberger, *Jesaja*, pp. 903, 904, 1008ff. In addition to Duhm, the two scholars who have argued most extensively against the inclusion of all or parts of ch. 27 are W. Rudolph (*Jes. 24–27*, pp. 55, 56) and W.E. March (*Two Prophetic Compositions*, pp. 173, 174); the following comment by M.-L. Henry (*Glaubenskrise*, p. 192) reflects the tendency of scholars to follow too quickly the lead of Duhm: 'Seit Duhm ist es eine in der Forschung weithin akzeptierte These, daß, abgesehen von der Problematik der Verse 25,10b-12, der Abschnitt 27,2-11 als Kompilation aus Material verschiedener Herkunft anzusehen ist, die Verse 27,12-13 hingegen als legitimer Schluß der Jesaja-apokalypse'. The few scholars who see 27.2-11 as an integral part of the composition are W. Gesenius (*Jesaia*, pp. 813ff.); P.L. Redditt (*Isa. 24–27*, pp. 134-40, 225, 226); E.J. Kissane (*Isaiah*, pp. 299-303); J. Lindblom (*Jes.-Apok.*, pp. 53ff.).

48. These three factors represent a composite picture derived from the criticisms of B. Duhm, W. Rudolph, and W.E. March.

49. Actually, March did not demonstrate that the language is significantly different. Note the following words from 27.2ff. which appear in the rest of the composition: *bywm hhw'*, *yhwh*, *nṣr*, *rg'*, *pgd*, *lylh*, *ly*, *m'wz*, *'sh*, *šlwm*, *tbl*, *rwḥ*, *qwm*, *'yr*, *bṣwrh*.

50. B. Duhm, *Jesaia*, p. 190.

51. For the most part, scholars have misinterpreted vv. 2-11. Instead of perceiving the theme of reunification which runs throughout this section, they have understood the veses to be focusing solely on the destruction of Judah, or the relationship of Judah to a foreign city (Kessler, Wildberger, and Plöger excepted). Consequently, I have decided that it would be pointless to respond to their objections based on a difference of theme.

52. W. Eichrodt, *Ezekiel* (OTL; Philadelphia: Westminster Press, 1970), pp. 513, 514. Eichrodt and Zimmerli (*Ezekiel, II*, p. 272) attribute both 37.1-14 and 15-23 to the prophet, Ezekiel.

53. Cf. our discussion of vv. 7-11.

54. Hos. 2.2. H.W. Wolff (*Hosea* [Hermeneia; Philadelphia: Fortress Press, 1974], pp. 24-27) maintains that Hos. 2.2 is authentic to the prophet Hosea.

Notes to Chapter 5

1. P. Hanson, *Dawn*, pp. 25, 26.
2. G.W. Anderson, 'Isaiah XXIV-XXVII Reconsidered', p. 123.
3. P. Hanson, *Dawn*, p. 29.

BIBLIOGRAPHY

Ackroyd, P. 'Criteria for the Maccabean Dating of Old Testament Literature', *VT* 3 (1953), pp. 113-32

—*Exile and Restoration*. OTL. Philadelphia: Westminster, 1968.

—'The Vitality of the Word of God in the Old Testament', *ASTI* 1 (1962), pp. 63-82.

Albright, W.F. 'Some Remarks on The Song of Moses in Deuteronomy XXXII', *VT* 9 (1959), pp. 340-52.

Alexander, J.A. *The Earlier Prophecies of Isaiah*. New York/London: Wiley and Putnam, 1846.

Alt, A. 'Die Rolle Samarias bei der Entstehung des Judentums', *Festschrift für O. Procksch zum sechzigsten Geburtstag*. Leipzig: Hinrichs, 1934, pp. 5-28.

Anderson, B.W. 'Exodus Typology in Second Isaiah', *Israel's Prophetic Heritage, Essays in Honor of James Muilenburg*. ed. B.W. Anderson and W. Harrelson, New York: Harper & Brothers, 1962, pp. 177-95.

Anderson, G.W. 'Isaiah XXIV - XXVII Reconsidered', *VTS* 9 (1963), pp. 118-26.

Arndt, W.F., and Gingrich, F.W. *A Greek—English Lexicon of the New Testament and Other Early Christian Literature*. Chicago: University of Chicago Press, 1957.

Aubert, L, 'Une première apocalypse, Esaïe 24-27', *ETR* 11 (1936), pp. 279-96.

—'Une première apocalypse, Esaïe 24-27', *ETR* 12 (1937), pp. 54-67.

Barr, J. *The Semantics of Biblical Language*. Oxford: Oxford University Press, 1961.

Barth, C.F. *Introduction to the Psalms*. trans. R.A. Wilson, New York: Scribner's Sons, 1966.

Bauckham, R.J. 'The Rise of Apocalyptic', *Themelios* 3 (1978), pp. 10-23.

Beker, J.C. *Paul The Apostle*. Philadelphia: Fortress, 1980.

Birkeland, H. 'The Belief in the Resurrection of the Dead in the Old Testament', *ST* 3/1 (1950), pp. 60-78.

Bohner, J. 'Zu Jes. 24-27', *ZAW* 22 (1902), pp. 332-34.

Bright, J. *A History of Israel*. 3rd edn; Philadelphia: Westminster Press, 1981; 1st edn, 1972.

—*Jeremiah*. AB. New York: Doubleday, 1965.

Brown, F., Driver, S.R., Briggs, C.A. *A Hebrew and English Lexicon of the Old Testament*. Oxford: Clarendon, 1907.

Brueggemann, W. 'Weariness, Exile and Chaos', *CBQ* 34 (1972), pp. 19-38.

Calvin, J. *Commentary on the Book of the Prophet Isaiah*, II. Grand Rapids: Eerdmans, 1948; 1st Latin edn, 1550.

Casanowicz, J.M. 'Note on Some Usages of *lkn*', *JAOS* 13 (1909-1911), pp. 343-46.

Cazelles, H. 'Qui aurait visé, à l'origine, Isaie II 2-5?', *VT* 30 (1980), pp. 409-20.

Cheyne, T.K. *The Book of Isaiah, Chronologically Arranged*. London: Macmillan, 1870.

—*Introduction to the Book of Isaiah*. London: A. & C. Black, 1895.

—*The Prophecies of Isaiah*, I, II; London: Kegan Paul, 1881.

Childs, B.S. 'The Enemy from the North and the Chaos Tradition', *JBL* 78 (1959), pp. 187-98.

Clements, R. *Isaiah 1-39*. The New Century Bible Commentary. Grand Rapids: Eerdmans, 1980.
—'The Prophecies of Isaiah and the Fall of Jerusalem in 587 B.C.', *VT* 30 (1980), pp. 421-36.
Coggins, R.J. 'The Problem of Is. 24-27', *ET* 90 (1979), pp. 328-33.
Cohn, R.L. *The Shape of Sacred Space: Four Biblical Studies*. AAR Studies in Religion 23; Chico: Scholars Press 1981.
Cross, F.M. *Canaanite Myth and Hebrew Epic*. Cambridge, MA: Harvard University Press, 1973.
Dahood, M. *Psalms*, I, II, III; AB; Garden City, N.Y.: Doubleday, 1970.
Davidson, R. 'Universalism in Second Isaiah', *SJT* 16 (1963), pp. 166-85.
Day, J. '*tl 'wrt* in Isaiah 26.19', *ZAW* 90 (1978), pp. 265-69.
Delitzsch, F. *Biblical Commentary on the Prophecies of Isaiah* I. Edinburgh: T. & T. Clark, 1894.
DeVries, S.J. *Yesterday, Today and Tomorrow*. Grand Rapids: Eerdmans, 1975.
Driver, G.R. 'Isaiah I-XXXIX: Textual and Linguistic Problems', *JSS* 13 (1968), pp. 36-57.
—'Linguistic and Textual Problems: Isaiah I-XXXIX', *JTS* 38 (1937), pp. 36-50.
—'Some Hebrew Verbs, Nouns, and Pronouns', *JTS* 30 (1928), pp. 371-78.
Driver, S.R. *A Treatise on the Use of Tenses in Hebrew*. Oxford: Clarendon, 1881.
Duhm, B. *Das Buch Jesaia*. Göttingen: Vandenhoeck & Ruprecht, 1892.
Ehrlich, A.B. *Randglossen zur Hebräischen Bibel*, IV. Leipzig: Hinrichs, 1912.
Eichhorn, I.G. *Die Hebräischen Propheten*, III. Göttingen: Vandenhoeck & Ruprecht, 1819.
Eichrodt, W. *Ezekiel*. OTL. Philadelphia: Westminster, 1970.
Eissfeldt, O. *The Old Testament, An Introduction*. New York: Harper & Row, 1965.
Elder, W. 'A Theological-Historical Study of Is. 24-27'. Unpublished Dissertation, Baylor University, 1974.
Emerton, J.A. 'A Textual Problem in Isaiah 25.2', *ZAW* 89 (1977), pp. 64-73.
Ewald, H. *Die Propheten des Alten Bundes*, III. Göttingen: Vandenhoeck & Ruprecht, 1868.
Fohrer, G. 'Der Aufbau der Apokalypse des Jesajabuchs, Jes. 24-27', *CBQ* 25 (1963), pp. 34-45.
—*Das Buch Jesaja*, II. Züricher Bibelkommentare; Zürich/Stuttgart: Zwingli, 1962.
Friedländer, M. *The Commentary of Ibn Ezra on Isaiah*, Vol. I. London: Society of Hebrew Literature, 1873.
Frost, S.R. *Old Testament Apocalyptic*. London: Epworth, 1952.
Gaster, T.H. *Thespis*. New York: Schuman, 1950.
Gemser, B. 'The *rîb*- or Controversy-pattern in Hebrew Mentality', *Wisdom in Israel and in the Ancient Near East*, *VTS* 3 (1955), pp. 120-37.
Gesenius, W., Kautzsch, E. *Hebrew Grammar*. Oxford: Clarendon, 1898.
—*Commentar über den Jesaia*. Leipzig: F.C.W. Vogel, 1821.
Gordon, C.H. *Ugaritic Textbook*. AO 38; Rome: Pontifical Biblical Institute, 1965.
Gray, G.B. *A Critical and Exegetical Commentary on the Book of Isaiah, I-XXVII*, I. ICC; Edinburgh: T. & T. Clark, 1912.
—'Critical Discussions. Isaiah 26; 25.1-5; 34.12-14', *ZAW* 31 (1911), pp. 111-27.
Gray, J. 'The Day of Yahweh in Cultic Experience and Eschatological Perspective', *SEÅ* 39 (1974), pp. 5-37.
—*The Legacy of Canaan. The Ras Shamra Texts and Their Relevance to the Old Testament*. Leiden: Brill, 1957.
Gressmann, H. *Der Messias*. Göttingen: Vandenhoeck & Ruprecht, 1929.

—*Der Ursprung der israelitisch-jüdischen Eschatologie*. FRLANT 6; Göttingen: Vandenhoeck & Reprechts 1905.

Gunkel, H. *Einleitung in die Psalmen, Die Gattungen der religiösen Lyrik Israels*. Göttingen: Vandenhoeck & Ruprecht, 1933.

—*Schöpfung und Chaos in Urzeit und Endzeit*. Göttingen: Vandenhoeck & Ruprecht, 1885.

Habets, G.N.W. *Die grosse Jesaja-Apokalypse (Jes. 24–27); Ein Beitrag zur Theologie des Alten Testament*. Bonn: Heerlen/Niederlande, 1974.

Hahnhart, R. 'Die jahwefeindliche Stadt', *Festschrift für W. Zimmerli*. BZAT, ed. H. Donner, R. Hahnhart, and R. Smend; Göttingen: Vandenhoeck & Ruprecht, 1977, pp. 152-63.

Hanson, P. 'Old Testament Apocalyptic Reexamined', *Interpretation* 25 (1971), pp. 454-79.

—*The Dawn of Apocalyptic, The Historical and Sociological Roots of Jewish Apocalyptic Eschatology*. Philadelphia: Fortress, 1979; 1st edn, 1975.

Hatch, E., Redpath, H.A. *A Concordance to the Septuagint and the Other Greek Versions of the Old Testament*, I. Oxford: Clarendon, 1875 (Graz, Austria: Akademische Druck- u. Verlagsanstalt, 1954).

Hayes, J.H. 'The Tradition of Zion's Inviolability', *JBL* 82 (1963), pp. 419-26.

—and J.M. Miller, eds., *Israelite and Judaean History*. OTL. Philadelphia: Westminster, 1977.

Henry, M.-L. *Glaubenskrise und Glaubensbewahrung in den Dichtungen der Jesaja-apokalypse*. BWANT 86; Stuttgart: W. Kohlhammer, 1967.

Hillers, D. 'Ritual Procession of the Ark and Psalm 132', *CBQ* 30 (1968), pp. 48-55.

—*Treaty-Curses and the Old Testament Prophets*. BO 16; Rome: Pontifical Biblical Institute, 1964.

Hitzig, F. 'Zur Wortkritik, A. Im Alten Testament', *ZwTh* 18 (1875), pp. 190-202.

Holladay, W.L. *Isaiah: Scroll of a Prophetic Heritage*. Grand Rapids: Eerdmans, 1978.

Hurvitz, A. *A Linguistic Study of the Relationship between the Priestly Source and the Book of Ezekiel*. CRB 20; Paris: Gabalda 1982.

Irwin, W.H. 'Syntax and Style in Isaiah 26', *CBQ* 41 (1979), pp. 240-58.

Jacob, E. 'Du premier au deuxième chant de la vigne du prophète Esaïe. Réflexions sur Esaie 27,2-5', *Wort—Gebot—Glaube, Beiträge zur Theologie des Alten Testaments, Walter Eichrodt zum 80. Geburtstag*. ed. J.J. Stamm, E. Jenni and H.J. Stoebe; AThANT 59; Zürich: Zwingli, 1970, pp. 325-30.

Johnson, D.G. 'The Structure and Meaning of Romans 11', *CBQ* 46 (1984), pp. 91-103.

Kaiser, O. *Isaiah 13- 39*. OTL. Philadelphia: Westminster, 1974.

Käsemann, E. *New Testament Questions of Today*. Philadelphia: Fortress, 1979.

Kessler, W. *Gott geht es um das Ganze. Jesaja 56–66 und Jesaja 24–27*. BAT 19; 1960.

Kissane, E.J. *The Book of Isaiah*, I. Dublin: Richview, 1941.

Kline, R. *Israel in Exile, A Theological Interpretation*. Philadelphia: Fortress, 1979.

Klopfenstein, M.A. *Scham und Schande nach dem Alten Testament*. AThANT 62; Zurich: Meier, 1972.

Knierim, R. 'The Vocation of Isaiah', *VT* 18 (1968), pp. 47-68.

Kraus, H.-J. *Die Königsherrschaft Gottes im Alten Testament*. BHT 13; Tübingen: Mohr, 1951.

Kugel, J.L. *The Idea of Biblical Poetry: Parallelism and its History*. New Haven and London: Yale University Press, 1981.

Liebmann, E. 'Der Text zu Jesaia 24–27', *ZAW* 22 (1902), pp. 1-56.
—'Der Text zu Jesaia 24–27', *ZAW* 23 (1903), pp. 209-86.
—'Der Text zu Jesaia 24–27', *ZAW* 24 (1904), pp. 51-104.
—'Der Text zu Jesaia 24–27', *ZAW* 25 (1905), pp. 145-71.
Lindblom, J. *Die Jesaja-Apokalypse, Jes. 24–27*. Lund: Gleerup, 1938.
Lohmann, P. 'Die selbständigen lyrischen Abschnitte in Jes. 24-27', *ZAW* 37 (1917), pp. 1-58.
—'Zu Text und Metrum einiger Stellen aus Jesaja', *ZAW* 33 (1913), pp. 251-64.
Lowth, R. *Isaiah: A New Translation*. Boston: Hillard, 1834.
McGuire, E.M. 'Yahweh and Leviathan, An Exegesis of Is. 27.1', *RQ* 13 (1970), pp. 168-79.
MacKenzie, R.A.F., S.J. 'The City and Israelite Religion', *CBQ* 25 (1963), pp. 60-70.
Mandelkern, S. *Veteris Testamenti Concordantiae Hebraicae Atque Chaldaicae*. Tel Aviv: Sumptibus Schocken Hierosolymis, 1978.
March, W.E. 'A Study of Two Prophetic Compositions in Is. 24.1–27.1'. Unpublished Dissertation, Union Theological Seminary, New York, 1966.
Martin-Achard, R. *From Death to Life; A Study of the Development of the Doctrine of the Resurrection in the Old Testament*. Edinburgh & London: Oliver & Boyd, 1960.
Mauchline, J. *Isaiah 1–39*. TBC. New York: Macmillan, 1962.
May, H.G. 'The Departure of the Glory of Yahweh', *JBL* 56 (1937), pp. 309-21.
Millar, W.R. *Isaiah 24–27 and the Origin of Apocalyptic*. Missoula, Montana: Scholars Press, 1976.
Mowinckel, S. *The Psalms in Israel's Worship*. trans. by D.R. Ap-Thomas; 2 vols.; New York: Abingdon, 1962.
Mulder, E.S. *Die Teologie van die Jesaja-apokalipse, Jesaja 24–27*. Groningen, Djakarta: J.B. Wolters, 1954.
Munch, P.A. *The Expression Bajjôm Hahû', Is it an Eschatological Terminus Technicus?* Avhandlingen utgitt av det Norske Videnskaps-Akademi i Oslo, 2, 1936.
Neusner, J. 'Judaism in a Time of Crisis, Four Responses to the Destruction of the Second Temple', *Judaism* 21 (1972), pp. 313-27.
Noth, M. *The History of Israel*. London: A. & C. Black, 1958.
O'Connor, M. *Hebrew Verse Structure*. Winona Lake, IN: Eisenbrauns, 1980.
Orlinsky, H.M. 'Nationalism–Universalism and Internationalism in Ancient Israel', *Translating and Understanding the Old Testament, Essays in Honor of H.G. May*. ed. H.T. Frank and W.L. Reed; New York: Abingdon, 1970.
Otzen, B. 'Traditions and Structures of Isaiah XXIV–XXVII', *VT* 24 (1974), pp. 196-206.
Pfeiffer, R.H. *Introduction to the Old Testament*. New York: Harper & Brothers, 1941.
Plöger, O. *Theocracy and Eschatology*. Richmond, Va.: John Knox Press, 1968, trans. from 1959 German edn.
Polzin, R. *Late Biblical Hebrew; Toward an Historical Typology of Biblical Hebrew Prose*. HSM 12; Missoula, Montana: Scholars Press, 1976.
Popper, W. 'Parallelism in Isaiah, Chapters 11–35', *University of California Publications in Semitic Philology* 1 (1923), pp. 445-552.
Pritchard, J.B. *The Ancient Near East, An Anthology of Texts and Pictures*, I; Princeton: Princeton University Press, 1969.
Procksch, O. *Jesaia*, I. KAT 9; Leipzig: Scholl, 1930.

Rad, G. von *Genesis*. OTL. Philadelphia: Westminster 1972.
—'The Origin of the Concept of the Day of Yahweh', *JSS* 4 (1959), pp. 97-108.
Redditt, P.L. 'Isaiah 24–27: A Form-Critical Analysis', Unpublished Dissertation, Vanderbilt University, 1972.
—'Postexilic Eschatological Prophecy and the Rise of Apocalyptic Literature', *OJRS* 2 (1974), pp. 25-39.
Ringgren, H. 'Some Observations on Style and Structure in the Isaiah Apocalypse', *ASTI* 9 (1973), pp. 107-15.
Roberts, J.J.M. 'Form, Syntax, and Redaction in Isaiah 1.2-20', *PSB* 3 (1982), pp. 293-306.
—'Isaiah in Old Testament Theology', *Interpretation* 36 (1982), pp. 130–43.
—'Zion Tradition', *IDBS*, pp. 985-87.
Robertson, E. 'Isaiah 27.2-6, an Arabic Poem?', *ZAW* 47 (1929), pp. 197-206.
Rost, L. 'Alttestamentliche Wurzeln der Ersten Auferstehung', *In Memoriam Ernst Lohmeyer*. ed. W. Schmauch; Stuttgart: Evangelisches Verlagswerk, 1951, pp. 67-72.
Rudolph, W. *Jesaja 24–27*. BWANT 9; Stuttgart: W. Kohlhammer, 1933.
Sawyer, J.F.A. *From Moses to Patmos*. London: SPCK, 1977.
Schmid, H.H. 'Schöpfung, Gerechtigkeit und Heil, "Schöpfungstheologie" als Gesamthorizont biblischer Theologie', *ZThK* (1970), pp. 1-19; ET 'Creation, Righteousness and Salvation, "Creation Theology" as the Broad Horizon of Biblical Theology', *Creation in the Old Testament*. ed. B.W. Anderson; Philadelphia: Fortress, 1984.
Schmidt, J. *Der Ewigkeitsbegriff im Alten Testament*. AA 13; Münster: Aschendorff, 1940.
Scott, Melville. *Textual Discoveries in Proverbs, Psalms and Isaiah*. London: SPCK, 1927.
Scott, R.B.Y. *Isaiah, 1–39*. The Interpreter's Bible, 5; Nashville: Abingdon, 1956.
Seeligmann, I.L. *The Septuagint Version of Isaiah, A Discussion of its Problems*. Leiden: Brill, 1948.
Smend, R. 'Anmerkungen zu Jes. 24–27', *ZAW* 4 (1884), pp. 161-224.
Smith, J.Z. 'Earth and Gods', *JR* 49 (1969), pp. 108-27
Spieckermann, H. *Juda unter Assur in der Sargonidenzeit*. Göttingen: Vandenhoeck & Ruprecht, 1982.
Stenning, J.F. *The Targum of Isaiah*. Oxford: Clarendon, 1949.
Stinespring, W.F. 'The Participle of the Immediate Future and Other Matters Pertaining to Correct Translation of the Old Testament', *Translating and Understanding the Old Testament, Essays in Honor of H.G. May*. ed. H.T. Frank and W.L. Reed; New York: Abingdon, 1970, pp. 64–70.
Tcherikover, V. *Hellenistic Civilization and the Jews*. New York: Atheneum, 1975.
Terrien, S. 'The Omphalos Myth and Hebrew Religion', *VT* 20 (1970), pp. 315-38.
Vatke, J.K.W. *Die Biblische Theologie wissenschaftlich dargestellt*. Berlin: G. Bethge, 1835.
Vawter, B. 'Apocalyptic: Its Relation to Prophecy', *CBQ* 22 (1960), pp. 33-46.
Vermeylen, J. *La composition littéraire de l'apocalypse d'Isaïe (Is., XXIV–XXVII)*. ALBO 5/14, 1974.
Wensinck, A.J. 'The Ocean in the Literature of the Western Semites', in *Studies of A.J. Wensinck*. New York: Arno, 1978.
Westermann, C. *Isaiah 40–66*. OTL. Philadelphia: Westminster, 1977, 1st German edition, 1966.

—*Praise and Lament in the Psalms*. trans. by K.R. Crim and R.N. Soulen, Atlanta: John Knox, 1981; 1st German edition, 1961.
Wijngaards, J. 'Death and Resurrection in Covenantal Context (Hos. VI,2)', *VT* 17 (1967), pp. 226-39.
Wildberger, H. 'Die Thronnamen des Messias, Jes. 9,5b', *TZ* 16 (1960), pp. 314-32.
—*Jesaja*. BKAT 10/2; Neukirchen-Vluyn: Neukirchener Verlag, 1978.
Williams, R.J. *Hebrew Syntax: An Outline*, 2nd edn; Toronto: University of Toronto Press, 1980.
Wolff, H.W. *Hosea*. Hermeneia; Philadelphia: Fortress, 1974.
Würthwein, E. *Der 'am ha'arez im Alten Testament*. BWANT 17; Stuttgart: W. Kohlhammer, 1936.
Young, E.J. *The Book of Isaiah*. NIC II; Grand Rapids: Eerdmans, 1969.
Ziegler, J. *Septuaginta; Vetus Testamentum Graecum Auctoritate*, XIV, *Isaias*. Göttingen: Vandenhoeck & Ruprecht, 1939.
Zimmerli, W. *Ezekiel*, II (chapters 25–48). Hermeneia; Philadelphia: Fortress, 1983.

Selected Texts

The Oxford Annotated Apocrypha of the Old Testament, ed. B.M. Metzger; New York: Oxford University Press, 1977.
Biblica Hebraica Stuttgartensia 7, D.W. Thomas, 1968.
The Dead Sea Scrolls of St. Mark's Monastery, Vol. I, The Isaiah Manuscript and the Habakkuk Commentary, ed. M. Burrows; New Haven: The American Schools of Oriental Research, 1950.
The Prophets, Nevi'im, A New Translation of the Holy Scriptures According to the Masoretic Text. Philadelphia: The Jewish Publication Society of America, 1978.

INDEXES

INDEX OF BIBLICAL REFERENCES

INDEX OF AUTHORS

JOURNAL FOR THE STUDY OF THE OLD TESTAMENT
Supplement Series

1 I, HE, WE AND THEY:
A LITERARY APPROACH TO ISAIAH 53
D.J.A. Clines

*2 JEWISH EXEGESIS OF THE BOOK OF RUTH
D.R.G. Beattie

*3 THE LITERARY STRUCTURE OF PSALM 2
P. Auffret

4 THANKSGIVING FOR A LIBERATED PROPHET:
AN INTERPRETATION OF ISAIAH CHAPTER 53
R.N. Whybray

5 REDATING THE EXODUS AND CONQUEST
J.J. Bimson

6 THE STORY OF KING DAVID:
GENRE AND INTERPRETATION
D.M. Gunn

7 THE SENSE OF BIBLICAL NARRATIVE I:
STRUCTURAL ANALYSES IN THE HEBREW BIBLE (2nd edition)
D. Jobling

*8 GENESIS 1-11: STUDIES IN STRUCTURE AND THEME
P.D. Miller

*9 YAHWEH AS PROSECUTOR AND JUDGE:
AN INVESTIGATION OF THE PROPHETIC LAWSUIT (RIB PATTERN)
K. Nielsen

10 THE THEME OF THE PENTATEUCH
D.J.A. Clines

*11 STUDIA BIBLICA 1978 I:
PAPERS ON OLD TESTAMENT AND RELATED THEMES
Edited by E.A. Livingstone

12 THE JUST KING:
MONARCHICAL JUDICIAL AUTHORITY IN ANCIENT ISRAEL
K.W. Whitelam

13 ISAIAH AND THE DELIVERANCE OF JERUSALEM:
A STUDY OF THE INTERPRETATION OF PROPHECY
IN THE OLD TESTAMENT
R.E. Clements

14 THE FATE OF KING SAUL:
AN INTERPRETATION OF A BIBLICAL STORY
D.M. Gunn

15 THE DEUTERONOMISTIC HISTORY
M. Noth

16 PROPHECY AND ETHICS:
ISAIAH AND THE ETHICAL TRADITIONS OF ISRAEL
E.W. Davies

17 THE ROLES OF ISRAEL'S PROPHETS
D.L. Petersen

18 THE DOUBLE REDACTION OF THE DEUTERONOMISTIC HISTORY
R.D.Nelson

19 ART AND MEANING: RHETORIC IN BIBLICAL LITERATURE
Edited by D.J.A. Clines, D.M. Gunn, & A.J. Hauser

20 THE PSALMS OF THE SONS OF KORAH
M.D. Goulder

21 COLOUR TERMS IN THE OLD TESTAMENT
A. Brenner

22 AT THE MOUNTAIN OF GOD:
STORY AND THEOLOGY IN EXODUS 32–34
R.W.L. Moberly

23 THE GLORY OF ISRAEL:
THE THEOLOGY AND PROVENIENCE OF THE ISAIAH TARGUM
B.D. Chilton

24 MIDIAN, MOAB AND EDOM:
THE HISTORY AND ARCHAEOLOGY OF LATE BRONZE AND IRON AGE
JORDAN AND NORTH-WEST ARABIA
Edited by J.F.A. Sawyer & D.J.A Clines

25 THE DAMASCUS COVENANT:
AN INTERPRETATION OF THE 'DAMASCUS DOCUMENT'
P.R. Davies

26 CLASSICAL HEBREW POETRY:
A GUIDE TO ITS TECHNIQUES
W.G.E. Watson

27 PSALMODY AND PROPHECY
W.H. Bellinger

28 HOSEA: AN ISRAELITE PROPHET IN JUDEAN PERSPECTIVE
G.I. Emmerson

29 EXEGESIS AT QUMRAN:
4QFLORILEGIUM IN ITS JEWISH CONTEXT
G.J. Brooke

30 THE ESTHER SCROLL: THE STORY OF THE STORY
D.J.A. Clines

31 IN THE SHELTER OF ELYON:
ESSAYS IN HONOR OF G.W. AHLSTRÖM
Edited by W.B. Barrick & J.R. Spencer

32 THE PROPHETIC PERSONA:
JEREMIAH AND THE LANGUAGE OF THE SELF
T. Polk

33 LAW AND THEOLOGY IN DEUTERONOMY
J.G. McConville

34 THE TEMPLE SCROLL:
AN INTRODUCTION, TRANSLATION AND COMMENTARY
J. Maier

35 SAGA, LEGEND, TALE, NOVELLA, FABLE:
NARRATIVE FORMS IN OLD TESTAMENT LITERATURE
Edited by G.W. Coats

36 THE SONG OF FOURTEEN SONGS
M.D. Goulder

37 UNDERSTANDING THE WORD:
ESSAYS IN HONOR OF BERNHARD W. ANDERSON
Edited by J.T. Butler, E.W. Conrad & B.C. Ollenburger

38 SLEEP, DIVINE AND HUMAN, IN THE OLD TESTAMENT
T.H. McAlpine

39 THE SENSE OF BIBLICAL NARRATIVE II:
STRUCTURAL ANALYSES IN THE HEBREW BIBLE
D. Jobling

40 DIRECTIONS IN BIBLICAL HEBREW POETRY
Edited by E.R. Follis

41 ZION, THE CITY OF THE GREAT KING:
A THEOLOGICAL SYMBOL OF THE JERUSALEM CULT
B.C. Ollenburger

42 A WORD IN SEASON: ESSAYS IN HONOUR OF WILLIAM McKANE
Edited by J.D. Martin & P.R. Davies

43 THE CULT OF MOLEK:
A REASSESSMENT
G.C. Heider

44 THE IDENTITY OF THE INDIVIDUAL IN THE PSALMS
S.J.L. Croft

45 THE CONFESSIONS OF JEREMIAH IN CONTEXT:
SCENES OF PROPHETIC DRAMA
A.R. Diamond

46 THE BOOK OF THE JUDGES: AN INTEGRATED READING
B.G. Webb

47 THE GREEK TEXT OF JEREMIAH:
A REVISED HYPOTHESIS
S. Soderlund

48 TEXT AND CONTEXT:
OLD TESTAMENT AND SEMITIC STUDIES FOR F.C. FENSHAM
Edited by W. Claassen

49 THEOPHORIC PERSONAL NAMES IN ANCIENT HEBREW
J.D. Fowler

50 THE CHRONICLER'S HISTORY
M. Noth

51 DIVINE INITIATIVE AND HUMAN RESPONSE IN EZEKIEL
P. Joyce

52 THE CONFLICT OF FAITH AND EXPERIENCE IN THE PSALMS:
A FORM-CRITICAL AND THEOLOGICAL STUDY
C.C. Broyles

53 THE MAKING OF THE PENTATEUCH:
A METHODOLOGICAL STUDY
R.N. Whybray

54 FROM REPENTANCE TO REDEMPTION:
JEREMIAH'S THOUGHT IN TRANSITION
J. Unterman

55 THE ORIGIN TRADITION OF ANCIENT ISRAEL:
THE LITERARY FORMATION OF GENESIS AND EXODUS 1–23
T.L. Thompson

56 THE PURIFICATION OFFERING IN THE PRIESTLY LITERATURE:
ITS MEANING AND FUNCTION
N. Kiuchi

57 MOSES: HEROIC MAN, MAN OF GOD
G.W. Coats

58 THE LISTENING HEART: ESSAYS IN WISDOM AND THE PSALMS
IN HONOR OF ROLAND E. MURPHY, O. CARM.
Edited by K.G. Hoglund

59 CREATIVE BIBLICAL EXEGESIS:
CHRISTIAN AND JEWISH HERMENEUTICS THROUGH THE CENTURIES
B. Uffenheimer & H.G. Reventlow

60 HER PRICE IS BEYOND RUBIES:
THE JEWISH WOMAN IN GRAECO-ROMAN PALESTINE
L.J. Archer

61 FROM CHAOS TO RESTORATION:
AN INTEGRATIVE READING OF ISAIAH 24–27
D.G. Johnson

62 THE OLD TESTAMENT AND FOLKLORE STUDY
P.G. Kirkpatrick

63 SHILOH: A BIBLICAL CITY IN TRADITION AND HISTORY
D.G. Schley

64 TO SEE AND NOT PERCEIVE:
ISAIAH 6.9-10 IN EARLY JEWISH AND CHRISTIAN INTERPRETATION
C.A. Evans

65 THERE IS HOPE FOR A TREE:
THE TREE AS METAPHOR IN ISAIAH
K. Nielsen

66 THE SECRETS OF THE TIMES:
RECOVERING BIBLICAL CHRONOLOGIES
J. Hughes

67 ASCRIBE TO THE LORD:
BIBLICAL AND OTHER ESSAYS IN MEMORY OF PETER C. CRAIGIE
Edited by L. Eslinger & G. Taylor

68 THE TRIUMPH OF IRONY IN THE BOOK OF JUDGES
L.R. Klein

69 ZEPHANIAH, A PROPHETIC DRAMA
P.R. House

70 NARRATIVE ART IN THE BIBLE
S. Bar-Efrat

71 QOHELET AND HIS CONTRADICTIONS
M.V. Fox

72 CIRCLE OF SOVEREIGNTY:
A STORY OF STORIES IN DANIEL 1–6
D.N. Fewell

73 DAVID'S SOCIAL DRAMA:
A HOLOGRAM OF THE EARLY IRON AGE
J.W. Flanagan

* Out of print